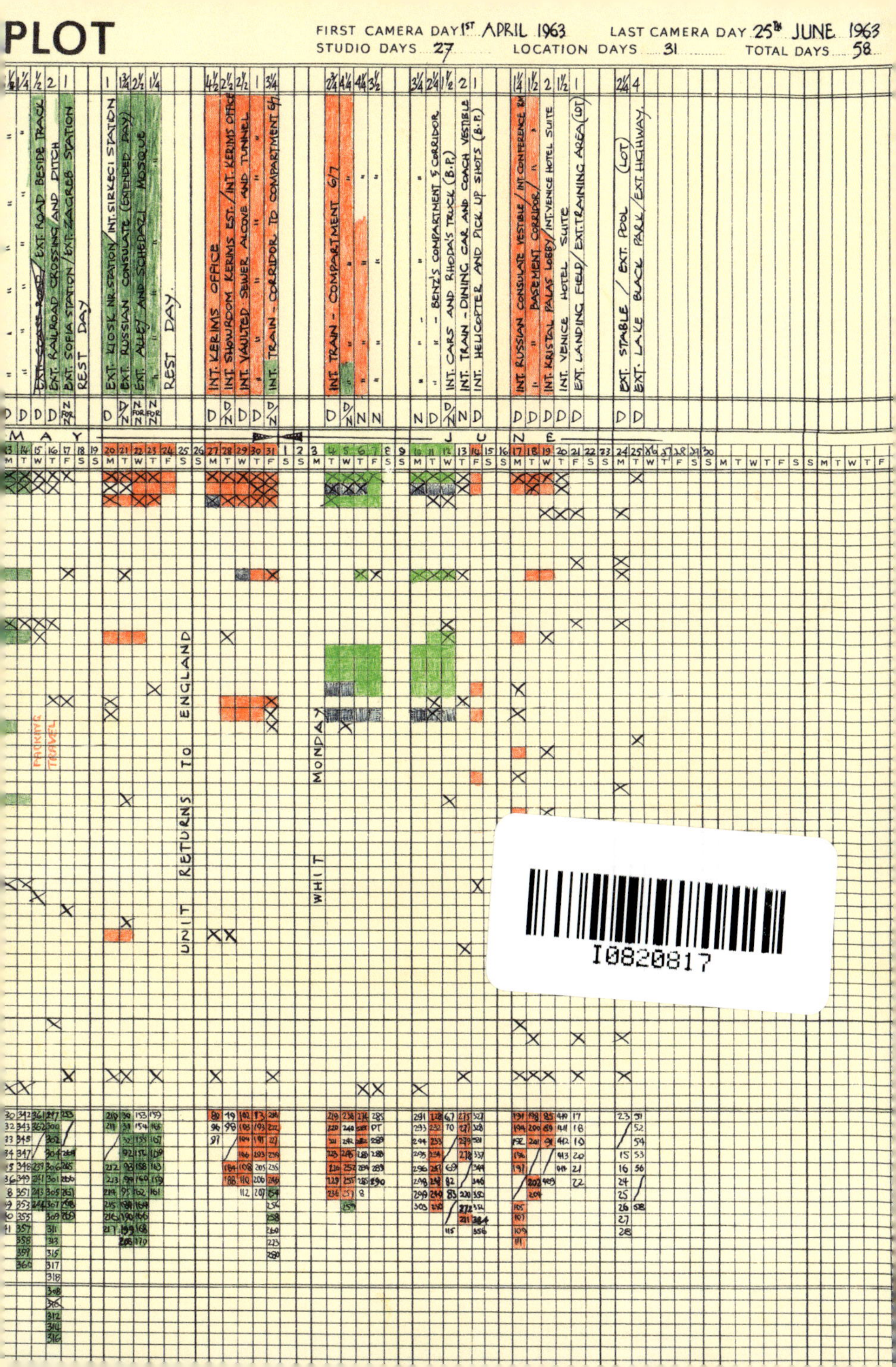

PLOT
FIRST CAMERA DAY 1ST APRIL 1963
LAST CAMERA DAY 25TH JUNE 1963
STUDIO DAYS 27
LOCATION DAYS 31
TOTAL DAYS 58
EXT. RAILROAD CROSSING AND DITCH
EXT. SOFIA STATION / EXT. ZAGREB STATION
REST DAY
EXT. KIOSK NR. STATION / INT. SIRKECI STATION
EXT. RUSSIAN CONSULATE (EXTENDED DAY)
EXT. ALLEY AND SCHEDAZI MOSQUE
REST DAY
INT. KERIMS OFFICE
INT. SHOWROOM KERIMS EST. / INT. KERIMS OFFICE
INT. VAULTED SEWER ALCOVE AND TUNNEL
INT. TRAIN - CORRIDOR TO COMPARTMENT 6/7
INT. TRAIN - COMPARTMENT 6/7
BENZ'S COMPARTMENT & CORRIDOR
INT. CARS AND RHODA'S TRUCK (B.P.)
INT. TRAIN - DINING CAR AND COACH VESTIBLE
INT. HELICOPTER AND PICK UP SHOTS (B.P.)
INT. RUSSIAN CONSULATE VESTIBLE / INT. CONFERENCE RM
BASEMENT CORRIDOR
INT. KRISTOL PALAS LOBBY / INT. VENICE HOTEL SUITE
INT. VENICE HOTEL SUITE
EXT. LANDING FIELD / EXT. TRAINING AREA (LOT)
EXT. STABLE / EXT. POOL (LOT)
EXT. LAKE BLACK PARK / EXT. HIGHWAY
MAY
JUNE
UNIT RETURNS TO ENGLAND
WHIT MONDAY
I0820817

THE JAMES BOND ARCHIVES

BY PAUL DUNCAN

THE COMPLETE FILMS

007™

TASCHEN

Contents

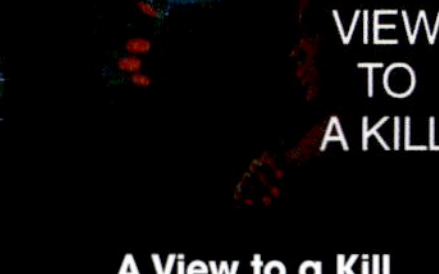

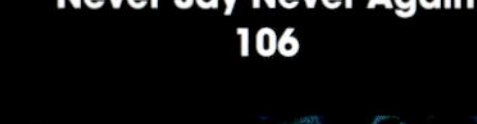

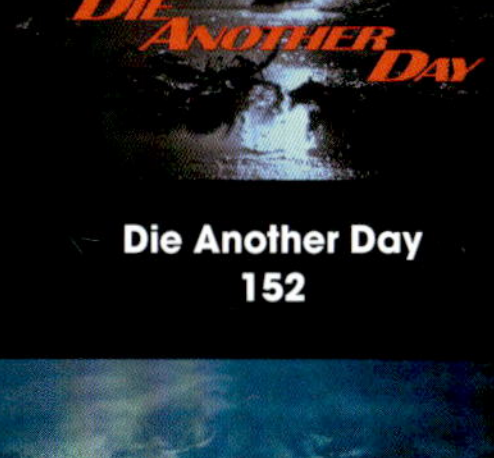

Introduction

By Paul Duncan

Exactly halfway through the first James Bond film, *Dr. No*, Bond prepares a trap for Professor Dent. Bond arranges a bedroom to make it look as though he is asleep in bed, then calmly puts a silencer on his gun, and plays a card game as he waits behind the doorway. Deep into the night, Dent carefully opens the bedroom door and empties his gun into the bed. Bond, knowing that Dent's gun is empty —"You've had your six," he says—shoots Dent in cold blood, then puts another round into Dent as he lies on the floor. Bond, still sitting, unscrews his silencer and blows into it, contemplating his next move.

This is the quintessential Bond moment. Up to this point, Bond has been a charming, cultivated gentleman, equally at home in a casino or a seafront bar, fully able to repel attacks from devious chauffeurs or rapacious women. And then he kills without hesitation, for Queen and Country. It is the first time that we understand what it means to have a license to kill.

Although the scene has no equivalent in the novel, it perfectly embodies the character of the literary James Bond created by Ian Fleming. Fleming began writing the first Bond novel, *Casino Royale*, at his Jamaican holiday home, Goldeneye, in February 1952. It was something that had been on his mind for some time. During World War Two, Fleming had been the personal assistant to Admiral John Godfrey, director of the Naval Intelligence Division of the Admiralty. He was an organizer and ideas man on a multitude of fronts, including the formation of 30 Assault Unit, information-gathering commandos who searched for and found vital German documents and equipment. In short, Fleming had been a spy. Prevented by the Official Secrets Act from talking about it openly, like spies before him and since—for example, W. Somerset Maugham (*Ashenden: Or the British Agent*) or John le Carré (*The Spy Who Came in from the Cold*)—he had turned to fiction. Through writing, Fleming could immerse himself in that world again, and relive the excitement of that secret life.

The Bond novels were successful, touching a chord in a generation of Britons who had lived through the war and wanted a more exotic international lifestyle rather than the austerity measures at home. It was only natural that such a charismatic character as James Bond would be adapted to other media like TV, comic strips, and film. Fleming, with his characteristic attention to detail, vetted each potential suitor. After a failed attempt to make a film with Ivar Bryce, Kevin McClory, and Ernest Cuneo, Fleming let producer Harry Saltzman option the Bond film and television rights. Saltzman's previous credits included the gritty dramas *Look Back in Anger*, *Saturday Night and Sunday Morning*, and *The Entertainer*. The films are serious-minded, documentary-tinged, psychologically complex pieces of filmmaking. If only a fraction of that attitude could be transferred into a Bond film, then there was the possibility that the character of Bond could be successfully adapted for the screen. However, Harry had a problem—he needed to find a studio and secure financing for the film.

For several years experienced film producer Albert R. "Cubby" Broccoli had been trying to secure the rights to the Bond novels without success. Through a mutual friend, Wolf Mankowitz, Harry Saltzman met Cubby Broccoli, and they agreed to go into business together making Bond movies as EON Productions. As cofounder of Warwick Films, from 1953 to 1960 Cubby had made over 20 action-adventure movies in the UK featuring top American stars. Cubby took Harry to meet United Artists, and they secured a deal for the Bond films within an hour. Cubby then assembled many of his crew and technicians from his Warwick days—screenwriter Richard Maibaum, director Terence Young, director of photography Ted Moore, production designer Ken Adam, stunt coordinator Bob Simmons, et al—and, together with Sean Connery as James Bond, EON Productions made the first James Bond movie, *Dr. No*, in 1962. I think it is fair to say that Ian Fleming's trust in Saltzman and Broccoli was well founded.

The James Bond Archives is an illustrated tour through *Dr. No*, and all the 007 movies that have followed over 60 years, including rare and unseen photographs and documents found in the official Bond archive. I was graciously allowed to look through over one million photos, and over 100 filing cabinets of production documentation, to make this book, and I hope that this book repays that trust.

The James Bond Archives is also a tribute to the film legacy that Cubby Broccoli and Harry Saltzman began, and that Cubby's stepson Michael G. Wilson and daughter Barbara Broccoli continued and evolved. Together these four producers had an incredible track record that no other production company can match—25 EON-produced films over seven decades and every one of them made a profit. It's no wonder that the James Bond franchise is still considered the gold standard by which other film franchises have to be compared.

Dr. No

1962

RELEASE DATE October 5, 1962 (UK) | **RUNNING TIME** 110 minutes

Synopsis

Arriving in Jamaica to investigate the suspected murder of a fellow agent and his secretary, James Bond eludes several attempts on his life. With the help of CIA agent Felix Leiter and local fisherman Quarrel, Bond follows the sinister trail of Dr. No to his island Crab Key. Shortly after landing on the beach with Quarrel, Bond encounters alluring shell collector Honey Ryder. The three uninvited visitors are hunted down by Dr. No's private army, who kill Quarrel then take Bond and Honey to Dr. No's magnificent lair.

Their megalomaniac host, Dr. No, tells Bond that by utilizing the nuclear laboratory on site, he plans to destroy the US Space program as his first move towards world domination. Bond outwits Dr. No who falls victim to his own scheme and dies.

Rescuing Honey, Bond commandeers a motorboat and together they escape from Crab Key, seconds before it explodes, leaving the final devastation of Dr. No's fantastic laboratory behind.

Cast

JAMES BOND SEAN CONNERY
HONEY RYDER URSULA ANDRESS
DR. JULIUS NO JOSEPH WISEMAN
FELIX LEITER JACK LORD
M BERNARD LEE
PROFESSOR R.J. DENT ANTHONY DAWSON
MISS TARO ZENA MARSHALL
QUARREL JOHN KITZMILLER

Crew

DIRECTOR TERENCE YOUNG
SCREENPLAY RICHARD MAIBAUM, JOHANNA M. HARWOOD, BERKELY MATHER
PRODUCERS HARRY SALTZMAN, ALBERT R. BROCCOLI
DIRECTOR OF PHOTOGRAPHY TED MOORE
PRODUCTION DESIGNER KEN ADAM

Now....meet the most extraordinary gentleman spy in all fiction.........

JAMES BOND

Agent 007...

!

THE FIRST JAMES BOND FILM ADVENTURE!

IAN FLEMING'S

Dr. No

007 THE DOUBLE "O" MEANS HE HAS A LICENSE TO KILL WHEN HE CHOOSES...WHERE HE CHOOSES...WHOM HE CHOOSES!

HARRY SALTZMAN and ALBERT R. BROCCOLI present IAN FLEMING'S Dr. No starring SEAN CONNERY as James Bond and URSULA ANDRESS JOSEPH WISEMAN JACK LORD also starring BERNARD LEE Screenplay by RICHARD MAIBAUM, JOHANNA HARWOOD, and BERKLEY MATHER Directed by TERENCE YOUNG Music Composed by MONTY NORMAN Produced by HARRY SALTZMAN and ALBERT R. BROCCOLI . EON PRODUCTIONS, LTD. TECHNICOLOR® Released thru UNITED UA ARTISTS

4

1. The iconic opening gun barrel and title sequences were created by Maurice Binder.

2. The American poster introduced the 007 logo, designed by Joseph Caroff, which is now recognized worldwide.

3. James Bond (Sean Connery) deals a card to Sylvia Trench (Eunice Gayson) in his first scene on the silver screen.

4. During the fight Connery flings stuntman Bob Simmons into the air.

5. Bond waits for Professor Dent (Anthony Dawson) at Miss Taro's house.

"To be candid, all the British actors I had interviewed, while very talented, lacked the degree of masculinity Bond demanded. To put it in the vernacular of our profession: Sean had the balls for the part."

—Cubby Broccoli, Producer

"The crew, the actors, everybody, we were like a big family. We were all equal, we were all together, we were all helping each other. It was camaraderie."

—Ursula Andress

6. Terence Young is under the camera directing John Kitzmiller, Ursula Andress, and Sean.

7. Dr. Julius No (Joseph Wiseman) trying to pull American missiles off course just prior to the Cuban missile crisis, when America and Russia almost went to war.

8. Chaos as Bond overloads the nuclear reactor. The machines were real or were based on real technology.

From Russia with Love

1963

RELEASE DATE October 10, 1963 (UK) | **RUNNING TIME** 115 minutes

Synopsis

James Bond is assigned by his superior, M, to help a young Russian girl, Tatiana Romanova, who has declared her desire to defect from her job as a clerk in the Russian embassy in Istanbul with an invaluable Lektor cipher machine.

Believing herself a willing tool of her government, Tatiana is actually the pawn of SPECTRE, a group of international criminals who plan to use the beautiful Russian girl to lure Bond to his death and to confound both the British and Russian Secret Service agencies.

In the intriguing atmosphere of Istanbul, Bond is aided by Kerim Bey, the Turkish agent for the British Secret Service, whom Bond comes to respect and admire. After eluding several death traps in Istanbul, Bond and Tatiana escape aboard the Orient Express.

SPECTRE has assigned their cold-blooded killer, Grant, to kill and discredit the famed British agent. In hand-to-hand combat, Bond triumphs over Grant in the close quarters of his train compartment, but the attempts on his life are by no means over.

He later fights an unequal battle against a SPECTRE helicopter and makes a desperate dash across the Gulf of Venice in a speedboat, chased by a horde of enemy agents. In Venice, he faces the final attempt on his life when Rosa Klebb, the master planner of the SPECTRE murder organization, makes a personal bid to kill him.

Cast

JAMES BOND SEAN CONNERY
TATIANA DANIELA BIANCHI
KERIM BEY PEDRO ARMENDÁRIZ
ROSA KLEBB LOTTE LENYA
GRANT ROBERT SHAW
M BERNARD LEE

Crew

DIRECTOR TERENCE YOUNG
SCREENPLAY RICHARD MAIBAUM
PRODUCERS HARRY SALTZMAN, ALBERT R. BROCCOLI
DIRECTOR OF PHOTOGRAPHY TED MOORE
TITLE SONG SUNG BY MATT MONRO

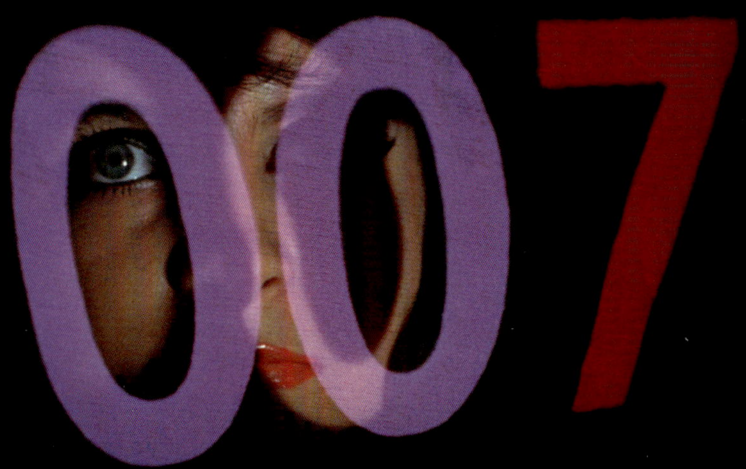

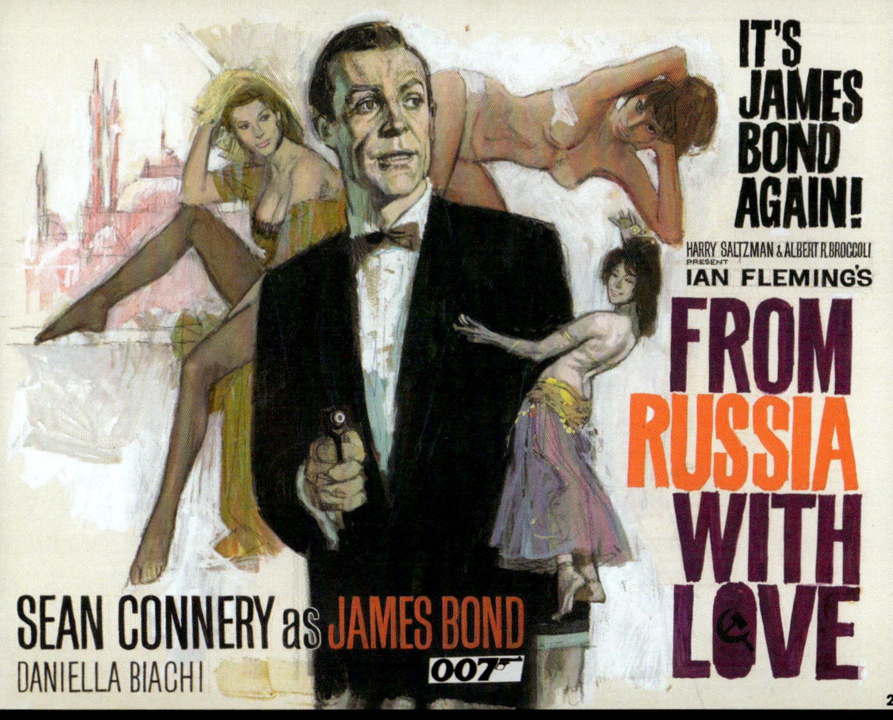

2

"It was the best of the Bond pictures. Not because I directed it, although I think it's well directed, but because it was the best subject for a Bond film."

4

1. This innovative title sequence was designed by Robert Brownjohn.

2. An unused poster design by Fratini.

3. SPECTRE assassin Red Grant (Robert Shaw) stalks and kills Bond with a garrote hidden in his watch.

4. Rosa Klebb (Lotte Lenya) recruits Tatiana Romanova (Daniela Bianchi) to seduce James Bond with both her body and the Lektor, the top-secret Russian encryption device.

"Everything on Bond is rather larger-than-life, so there are no little fight scenes. They're all blown up into something quite extravagant, and that's what made it all such fun."

—Richard Graydon, Stuntman

5. Tatiana introduces herself to Bond. Daniela's hairstyle indicates that this shot is from the first filming of the scene, before it was completely re-written and reshot.

6. After an epic fight, Bond strangles Grant with his own garrote.

"The feeling on the film was always good. Terence, who was the leader of the whole thing, was a wonderful personality and managed to instill into everybody an enthusiasm and a joy for making the film."

—Peter Hunt, Editor

6

7

"It's very difficult to do what Sean did, throwing those lines away. People say, 'Well, he just walked through it.' I think you're underestimating Sean as an actor. Sean made them work."

—John Barry, Composer

7. Bond is attacked by a SPECTRE helicopter. The weather was so bad that Terence Young had to improvise shots, and left it to Peter Hunt to edit them together as best he could.

8. As Rosa Klebb attacks Bond, Tatiana must decide whom to shoot.

9. The deadly dagger boot, worn by Rosa Klebb.

8

9

Goldfinger

1964

RELEASE DATE September 17, 1964 (UK) | **RUNNING TIME** 110 minutes

Synopsis

James Bond is assigned to investigate one of the wealthiest men in the world, Auric Goldfinger, who is suspected of smuggling England's gold reserves. Goldfinger's greed is exceeded only by his disrespect for human life. When his secretary Jill sleeps with Bond, after Bond catches him cheating at cards, Goldfinger has her killed by smothering her with gold paint. The dead girl's sister is also killed, when she follows Goldfinger to Switzerland and attempts revenge.

Bond is captured by Goldfinger's huge manservant Oddjob, and almost killed by a deadly laser beam. Drugged, he finds himself on Goldfinger's private jet being flown to America by Pussy Galore. Bond wins over Pussy and she helps thwart Goldfinger's plot to rob Fort Knox.

Cast

JAMES BOND SEAN CONNERY
PUSSY GALORE HONOR BLACKMAN
AURIC GOLDFINGER GERT FRÖBE
JILL MASTERSON SHIRLEY EATON
TILLY MASTERSON TANIA MALLET
ODDJOB HAROLD SAKATA
M BERNARD LEE

Crew

DIRECTOR GUY HAMILTON
SCREENPLAY RICHARD MAIBAUM, PAUL DEHN
PRODUCERS HARRY SALTZMAN, ALBERT R. BROCCOLI
DIRECTOR OF PHOTOGRAPHY TED MOORE
PRODUCTION DESIGNER KEN ADAM
MUSIC JOHN BARRY
TITLE SONG SUNG BY SHIRLEY BASSEY

ショーン・コネリー／
オナー・ブラックマン■ゲルト・フレーベ■監督ガイ・ハミルトン
シャーリー・イートン■タニア・マレット■音楽モンティー・ノーマン
全世界アクション・ファンの拍手を浴びて最大の危機に挑む─颯爽ジェームズ・ボンド！
007
ジェームズ・ボンドシリーズ第3作
総天然色
ゴールドフィンガー
SEAN
CONNERY
in IAN FLEMING'S AS AGENT 007 "GOLDFINGER"
原作イアン・フレミング
《早川書房刊》
ユナイト映画

CONFERENCE FEBRUARY 3rd: CONNERY, BROCCOLI, MAIBAUM

(1) Connery feels tone of script all wrong. Wants serious approach with humor interjected subtly as in other films.

(2) Feels that Bond's involvement with Goldfinger in Miami is too casual. He should be starting his investigation of Goldfinger there after finishing assignment in South America.

(3) He feels present script has lost Bond's mission, which was to find Goldfinger's gold hoard of twenty million pounds. That is why he goes along with Ft. Knox hoping continued association with Goldfinger will give him lead to the gold illegally smuggled out of England. Otherwise why doesn't he just shoot him ?

(4) Connery also feels that Bond should convince Goldfinger he is a criminal. Suggests (independent of first script which he says he never read) that bogus background be prepared for Bond which Goldfinger "discovers". However, Cubby replied that this was dubious as the "hostage" idea seems to work.

(5) Connery is very much against Pussy bouncing him around. He said make something out of their relationship or drop her out of the script.

(6) He hates scene in hay while Oddjob watches hay fall from loft.

(7) He thinks (this goes back to conception of Bond with a bogus criminal past) that Goldfinger should make Bond "prove" himself somehow. Perhaps by killing someone.

(8) He agrees that the authorities would have no reason to hold off springing their trap at Ft. Knox until the moment when they do in the present script unless an atomic device was involved. A particularly dirty bomb which they must get their hands on.

He feels that Bond is overshadowed completely by Goldfinger throughout the script and is especially disturbed by the ending. Bond does nothing to kill Goldfinger with whom he has a particularly nasty score to settle because of the two girls Goldfinger has had killed.

He thinks squeezing the golf ball is ludicrous.

He thinks the gangsters at the Stud Farm are Guys and Dolls characters. Instead they should be real menaces.

He dislikes theatre curtains and bodies routine at end.

He feels Goldfinger and Bond, as characters, should be more as they are in book. Thinks script is in bits and pieces and not "full", so far as playing scenes are involved.

He scoffed at Bond's leaving notes in vet's pill bottles. Thinks he must get word out to Leiter in some clever dangerous way.

Scene with Bond on mike during card game ineffectual.

Oddjob – Hits him

3

1. Images from Robert Brownjohn's innovative title sequence.

2. The Japanese film poster.

3. Cubby Broccoli and screenwriter Richard Maibaum met with Sean Connery in Los Angeles and listed his comments about the third draft of the script.

4. Bond discovers Jill Masterson (Shirley Eaton) dead—Goldfinger's revenge for her betrayal.

5. Paul Rabiger applies gold paint to Shirley Eaton.

4

"I always think of Goldfinger being almost the perfect Bond film."

—Michael G. Wilson, Producer

6. Filming on location at the Furka Pass, Switzerland.

7. Bond has to think his way out of danger in the Laser Room. Auric Goldfinger (Gert Fröbe) leaves Bond to his fate.

8. Ken Adam's design for the Laser Room.

"Sean was very much aware of the real dangers involved in making these types of pictures."

— Ken Adam, Production Designer

7

8

"Pussy Galore was girl power, let's face it."

—Honor Blackman

9

9. Pussy Galore (Honor Blackman) is introduced as a strong, no-nonsense woman who can hold any man at bay, even James Bond.

10. Only Bond's quick thinking results in Oddjob's (Harold Sakata) defeat.

11. Director Guy Hamilton (left) oversees the bomb's defusion.

Thunderball

1965

RELEASE DATE December 9, 1965 (Japan) | **RUNNING TIME** 130 minutes

Synopsis

SPECTRE steals a Vulcan bomber carrying two nuclear warheads and holds NATO to ransom to the sum of £100 million. In a race against time, Bond discovers the only lead—a photo of NATO pilot Major Derval with his sister, Domino—and is assigned to Nassau to investigate. Once he contacts Domino, and sees her connection to Emilio Largo, Bond and his team hunt for the bombs on board Largo's yacht, the Disco Volante, and at his villa, Palmyra, but without success.

After dispatching SPECTRE agent Fiona Volpe, Bond enlists the help of Domino by showing her proof that Largo killed her brother. As the Disco Volante sails for Miami with the bombs aboard, Domino is discovered spying and is tortured by Largo. Bond takes part in the thrilling underwater fight between SPECTRE and US aqua-paratroops, before tackling Largo on board the Disco Volante. As Largo is about to shoot Bond, Domino harpoons him, gaining revenge for the murder of her brother.

Cast

JAMES BOND SEAN CONNERY
DOMINIQUE "DOMINO" DERVAL CLAUDINE AUGER
EMILIO LARGO ADOLFO CELI
FIONA VOLPE LUCIANA PALUZZI
FELIX LEITER RIK VAN NUTTER
COUNT LIPPE GUY DOLEMAN
PATRICIA FEARING MOLLY PETERS

Crew

DIRECTOR TERENCE YOUNG
SCREENPLAY RICHARD MAIBAUM, JOHN HOPKINS
BASED ON THE ORIGINAL STORY BY KEVIN MCCLORY, JACK WHITTINGHAM, IAN FLEMING
PRODUCER KEVIN MCCLORY
EXECUTIVE PRODUCERS HARRY SALTZMAN, ALBERT R. BROCCOLI
DIRECTOR OF PHOTOGRAPHY TED MOORE
TITLE SONG SUNG BY TOM JONES

HERE COMES THE BIGGEST BOND OF ALL!

ALBERT R. BROCCOLI and HARRY SALTZMAN present

SEAN CONNERY

in IAN FLEMING'S "THUNDERBALL"

CLAUDINE AUGER · ADOLFO CELI
LUCIANA PALUZZI

Produced by KEVIN McCLORY Directed by TERENCE YOUNG Screenplay by RICHARD MAIBAUM and JOHN HOPKINS

Based on an original story by KEVIN McCLORY, JACK WHITTINGHAM and IAN FLEMING PANAVISION® TECHNICOLOR® Released thru UNITED ARTISTS

BMT 216A

4

1. The title sequence was shot by Maurice Binder starting on July 6, 1965, for three days, in the water tank at Pinewood. The water was heated overnight to keep the girls warm.

2. Bob McGinnis, a paperback-cover artist whose specialty was depicting beautiful women, used reference photos to paint the bottom third of the poster, while Frank McCarthy, who was a great adventure artist, painted the top two-thirds.

3. The force of the jet pack can be seen whipping the dust and stones off the road as it comes in to land. Waiting at the Aston Martin DB5 is French spy Madame LaPorte, played by Mitsouko.

5

6

4. Storyboards for the first meeting of Bond and Domino, François Derval's sister, which takes place underwater in the Bahamas.

5. Domino (Claudine Auger) swimming with the sea turtle.

6. Bond sucks the poison out of Domino's foot after she steps on a sea urchin.

"In a Bond film you aren't involved in cinéma vérité or avant-garde. One is involved in colossal fun."

—Terence Young

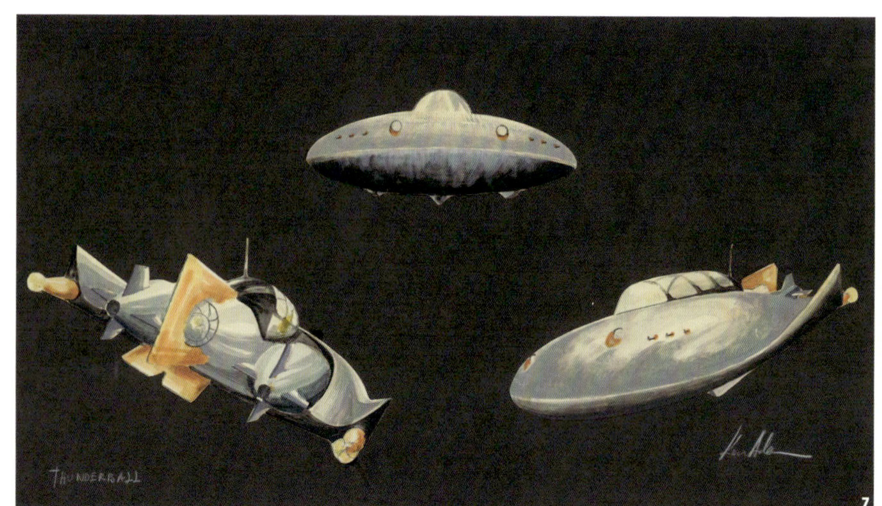

7

8

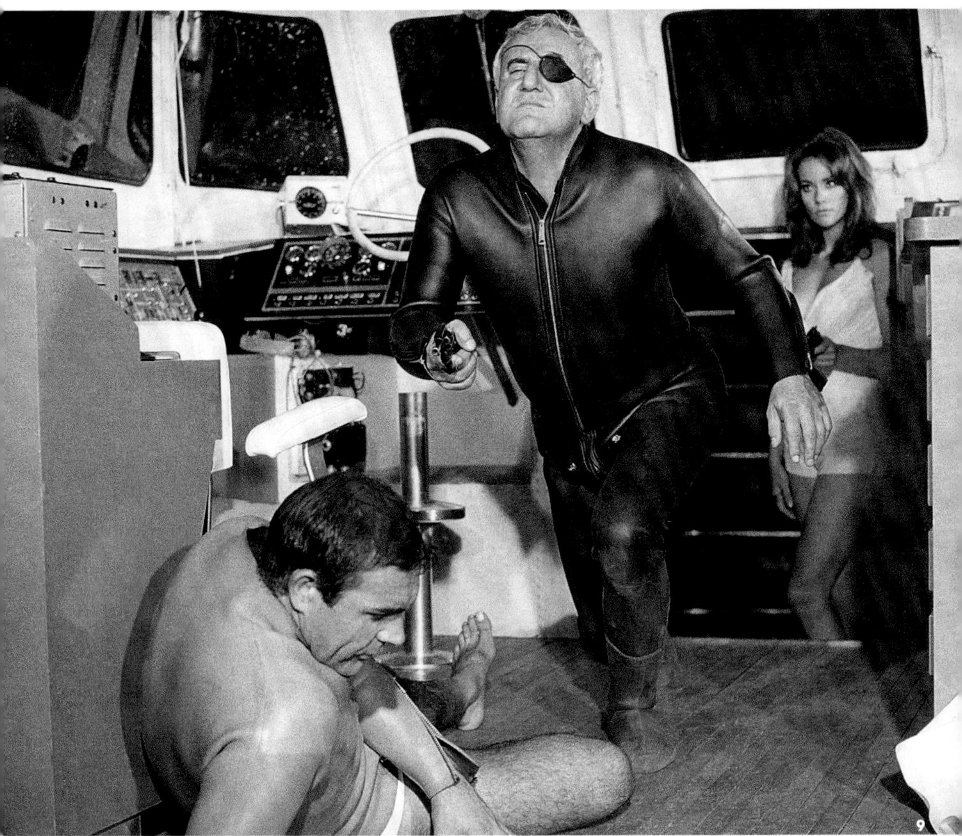

9

"My problem with* Thunderball *was to somehow rescue Bond from the machines."

—Terence Young

7. Ken Adam's design for the underwater bomb carrier. Ken Adam: "I thought nobody could ever realize these designs and that they weren't practical."

8. The underwater bomb carrier, built by Jordan Klein, in operation.

9. As Emilio Largo (Adolfo Celi) is about to shoot Bond, Domino harpoons Largo in the back—payback for the death of her brother.

Casino Royale

1967

RELEASE DATE April 14, 1967 (UK) | **RUNNING TIME** 131 minutes

Synopsis

Sir James Bond comes out of retirement to investigate the death of M. At M's ancestral home in Scotland, Bond is seduced by M's wife—in fact, Agent Mimi, working for SMERSH—and then survives an attack from remote-controlled exploding grouse.

Taking over as M, Sir James recruits several people to become James Bond 007. Moneypenny recruits Cooper as James Bond, who builds up his resistance to women by fighting The Detainer, who is also James Bond. Sir James recruits his daughter Mata Bond to infiltrate International Mother's Help in East Berlin. Expert baccarat player Evelyn Tremble becomes James Bond and works with Vesper Lynd to play Le Chiffre at Casino Royale. Le Chiffre loses, but kidnaps Tremble to recoup the money and allay the suspicions of his SMERSH boss, Dr. Noah.

All the Bonds end up at SMERSH's underground lair, where Dr. Noah is revealed to be Sir James's nephew Jimmy Bond. The final fight in Casino Royale is cut short when Jimmy Bond explodes, killing everybody.

Cast

EVELYN TREMBLE / JAMES BOND 007 PETER SELLERS
VESPER LYND / JAMES BOND 007 URSULA ANDRESS
SIR JAMES BOND DAVID NIVEN
LE CHIFFRE ORSON WELLES
MATA BOND JOANNA PETTET
THE DETAINER / JAMES BOND 007 DALIAH LAVI

Crew

DIRECTORS JOHN HUSTON, KEN HUGHES, VAL GUEST, ROBERT PARRISH, JOSEPH MCGRATH
SCREENPLAY WOLF MANKOWITZ, JOHN LAW, MICHAEL SAYERS
PRODUCERS CHARLES K. FELDMAN, JERRY BRESLER
DIRECTOR OF PHOTOGRAPHY JACK HILDYARD

1

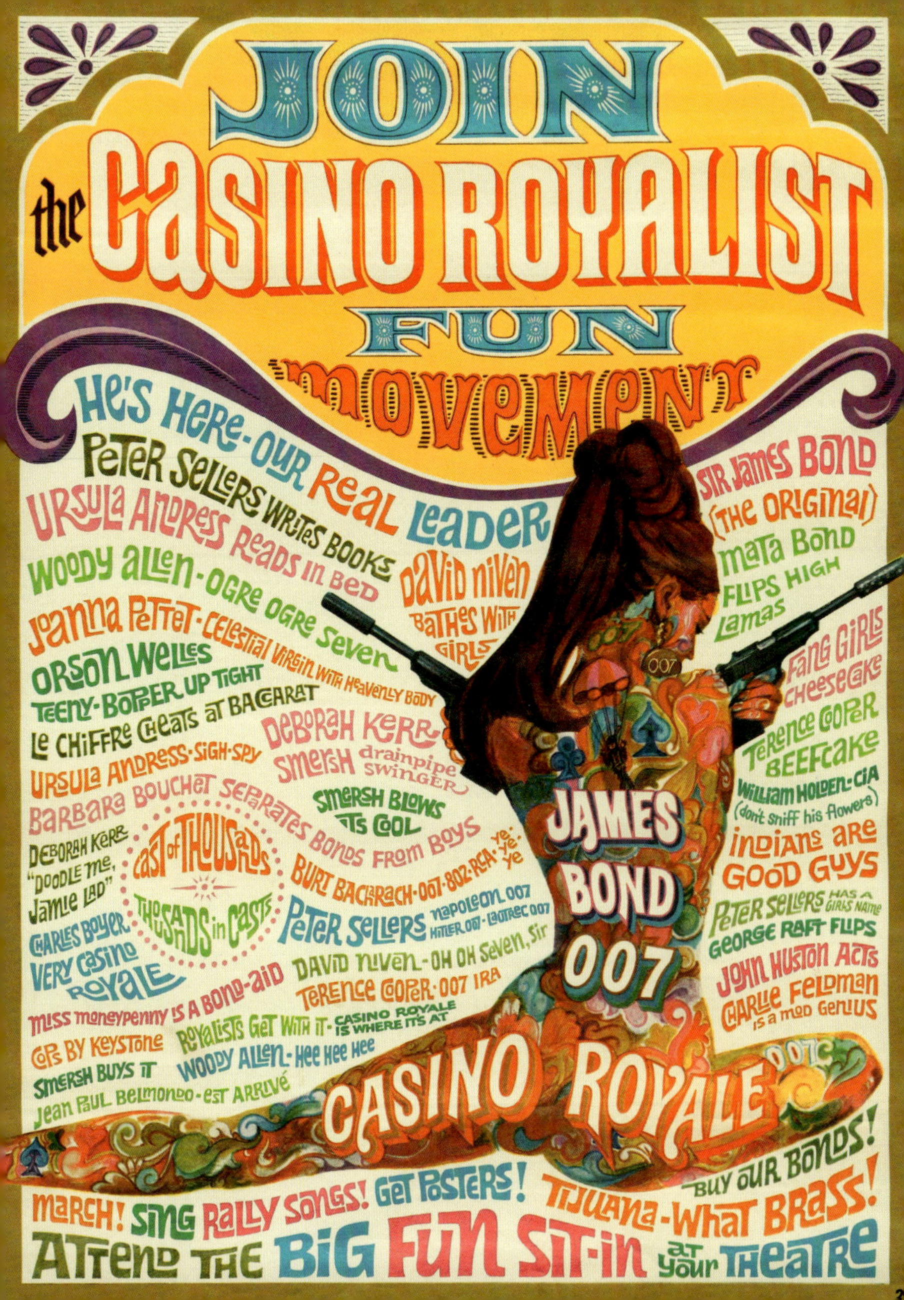
JOIN
the CASINO ROYALIST
FUN
MOVEMENT
HE'S HERE - OUR REAL LEADER
PETER SELLERS WRITES BOOKS
URSULA ANDRESS READS IN BED
WOODY ALLEN - OGRE OGRE SEVEN
JOANNA PETTET - CELESTIAL VIRGIN WITH HEAVENLY BODY
ORSON WELLES
TEENY-BOPPER UP TIGHT
LE CHIFFRE CHEATS AT BACCARAT
URSULA ANDRESS - SIGH-SPY
BARBARA BOUCHET SEPARATES BONDS FROM BOYS
DEBORAH KERR "DOODLE ME, JAMIE LAD"
CAST OF THOUSANDS
THOUSANDS IN CASTS
CHARLES BOYER VERY CASINO ROYALE
MISS MONEYPENNY IS A BOND-AID
COPS BY KEYSTONE
SMERSH BUYS IT
JEAN PAUL BELMONDO - EST ARRIVÉ
ROYALISTS GET WITH IT - CASINO ROYALE IS WHERE ITS AT
WOODY ALLEN - HEE HEE HEE
DAVID NIVEN - OH OH SEVEN, SIR
TERENCE COOPER - 007 IRA
PETER SELLERS NAPOLEON 007 HITLER 007 - LAUTREC 007
BURT BACHARACH - 007-802-RCA - YE, YE, YE
SMERSH BLOWS ITS COOL
DEBORAH KERR - SMERSH DRAINPIPE SWINGER
DAVID NIVEN BATHES WITH GIRLS
SIR JAMES BOND (THE ORIGINAL)
MATA BOND FLIPS HIGH LAMAS
FANG GIRLS CHEESECAKE
TERENCE COOPER BEEFCAKE
WILLIAM HOLDEN - CIA (don't sniff his flowers)
INDIANS ARE GOOD GUYS
PETER SELLERS HAS A GIRLS NAME
GEORGE RAFT FLIPS
JOHN HUSTON ACTS
CHARLIE FELDMAN IS A MOD GENIUS
JAMES BOND 007
CASINO ROYALE
MARCH! SING RALLY SONGS! GET POSTERS! TIJUANA - WHAT BRASS! BUY OUR BONDS!
ATTEND THE BIG FUN SIT-IN AT YOUR THEATRE

1. The Detainer (Daliah Lavi) is captured by Dr. Noah (Woody Allen). Detainer: "Do you treat all the girls you desire this way?" Noah: "Yes, I undress them and tie them up. I learned that in the Boy Scouts."

2. A rare poster for the film, which cost $12 million, and made $41.7 million worldwide.

3. Ursula Andress plays Vesper Lynd. Peter Sellers and writer Wolf Mankowitz read the script to her in her living room: "So finally I said yes."

4. The final fight was directed by Richard Talmadge. John Richardson: "Dick was one of the old, legendary Hollywood stuntmen, and he wanted to do all sorts of bizarre things like firing flaming arrows into a crowd of extras. We had bubble machines that covered everything with soap, so that everybody was slipping and sliding everywhere. We had seals. We had horses galloping up and down the stairs. We had giraffes standing at the bar. The whole thing was outrageous."

5. The casino office is full of Bonds: Cooper (Terence Cooper), Moneypenny (Barbara Bouchet), Mata (Joanna Pettit), Sir James (David Niven), and The Detainer. Sir James renames every spy "James Bond 007" to confuse the enemy.

6. Evelyn (Peter Sellers) and Vesper (left) watch as Le Chiffre (Orson Welles, right in white jacket) performs a magic trick. John Richardson: "Neither Orson nor Peter Sellers wanted to work on the set together. So they shot everything looking one way one day and everything looking the other way the next day. Peter would come in the morning with a script that he'd rewritten overnight, and then, the following day, Orson would come in and he'd rewritten his bit. Somehow it all went together at the end of the day. Goodness knows how."

4

"I never had so much fun in my life as making this film. It has been the first occasion I've been able to put together a high burlesque for the screen and it was a lark from beginning to end!"

—John Huston, Director

5

You Only Live Twice

1967

RELEASE DATE June 12, 1967 (UK) | **RUNNING TIME** 117 minutes

Synopsis

James Bond is assassinated by Chinese agents in Hong Kong, but it is a ruse so that Bond can travel incognito to Japan and investigate the hijacking of American and Russian spacecraft. Together with Tiger Tanaka and Aki of the Japanese secret service, Bond traces a supply of liquid oxygen, which is used to fuel rockets, to a southern Japanese island.

So that Bond can live on the island without arousing suspicion, he becomes Japanese in appearance, trains with Tanaka's ninjas, and marries Kissy Suzuki. Bond and Kissy look into the mysterious death of a fishing girl, and discover that SPECTRE, commanded by Ernst Stavro Blofeld, have a secret rocket complex hidden inside a volcano. Bond, Tanaka, Kissy, and the ninjas attack the base, and stop Blofeld from detonating a nuclear war between Russia and America, but Blofeld escapes, leaving the base to self-destruct.

Cast

JAMES BOND SEAN CONNERY
AKI AKIKO WAKABAYASHI
KISSY MIE HAMA
TIGER TANAKA TETSURO TAMBA
MR. OSATO TERU SHIMADA
HELGA BRANDT KARIN DOR
BLOFELD DONALD PLEASENCE

Crew

DIRECTOR LEWIS GILBERT
SCREENPLAY ROALD DAHL
PRODUCERS HARRY SALTZMAN, ALBERT R. BROCCOLI
DIRECTOR OF PHOTOGRAPHY FREDDIE YOUNG
PRODUCTION DESIGNER KEN ADAM
TITLE SONG SUNG BY NANCY SINATRA

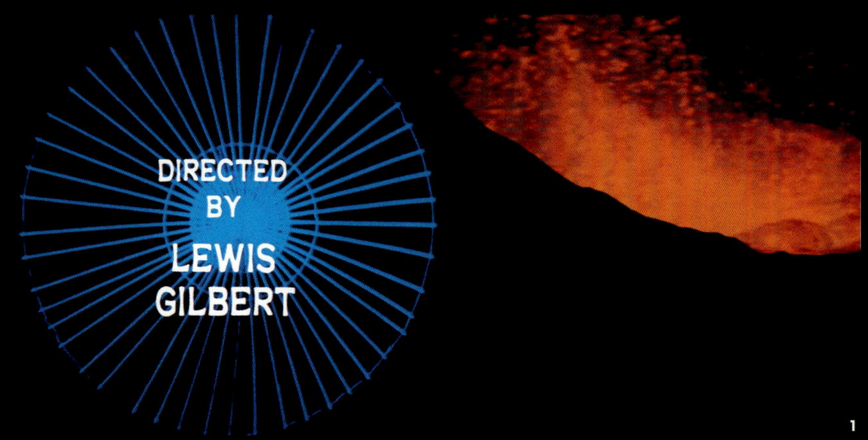

■AGENT 007
ショーン・コネリー
空前のスケールに昇奮3倍！アクションさえて迫力4倍！ボンドシリーズ第5弾！
♥ボンド・ガールズ♥浜 美枝／若林映子／カリン・ドール／ルイス・マクスウェル
ドナルド・プリーゼンス／丹波哲郎
■原作イアン・フレミング
監督ルイス・ギルバート
007
テクニカラー■パナビジョン
は二度死ぬ
SEAN CONNERY IS JAMES BOND IN IAN FLEMING'S "YOU ONLY LIVE TWICE"
映倫
UNITED ARTISTS
ユナイト映画

1. The title sequence was shot by Maurice Binder, who used footage from Haroun Tazieff's volcano documentary *Les Rendez-vous du diable* (1960) in the background.

2. The Japanese poster.

3. These storyboards helped the aerial unit visualize the fight between "Little Nellie" and the SPECTRE helicopters. Ken Adam: "I came up with making it look like a wasp, painting it yellow with black-and-white stripes."

4. Close-ups of Bond and the weapons in action were filmed at Pinewood in front of a blue screen. The flame gun shown was so hot that it damaged the camera lens.

5. Donald Pleasence glowers menacingly on set as Blofeld. He was brought in at the last minute to replace Jan Werich, who fell ill.

6. The volcano set is lit by a wall of lights on the left, as crew and visitors stand in the foreground out of shot.

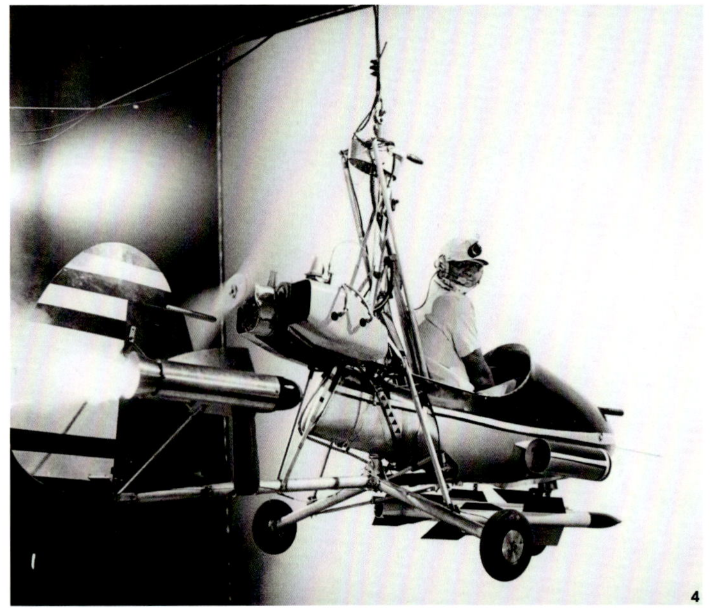

4

Bonds P.o.v. of THE Volcano.
213a) Circles rim of Volcano
213 b) Starts to climb
3

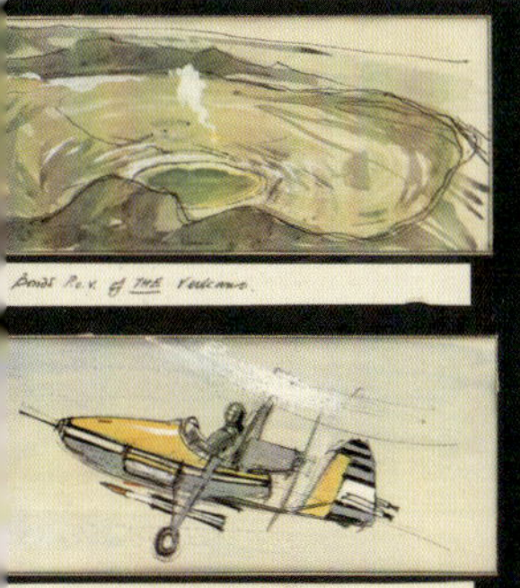

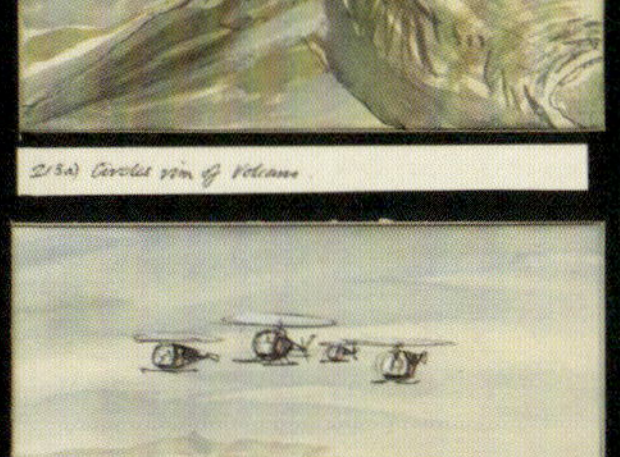

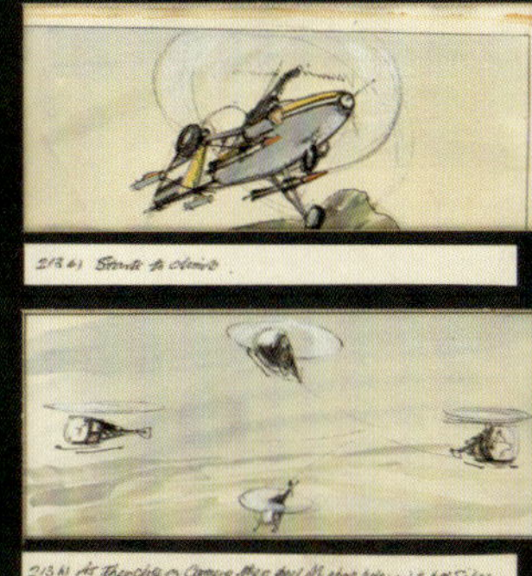

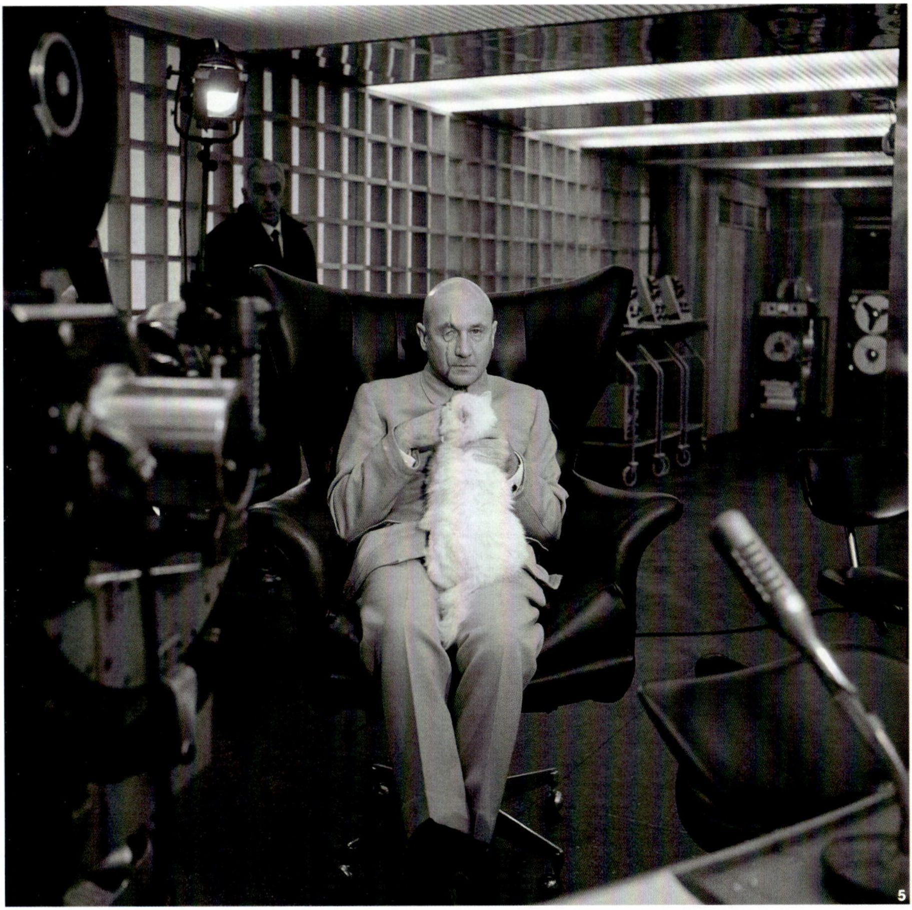
5

On Her Majesty's Secret Service

1969

RELEASE DATE December 18, 1969 (UK) | **RUNNING TIME** 142 minutes

Synopsis

While James Bond is hunting Ernst Stavro Blofeld, head of SPECTRE, at a beach he saves Tracy from committing suicide by drowning. Afterwards Bond and Tracy begin a relationship that gives her a reason to live. With the help of Tracy's father, Draco, head of the Unione Corse crime syndicate, Bond tracks down Blofeld to Piz Gloria, on a mountaintop in the Alps.

Here he finds that Blofeld is brainwashing a group of women to act as his secret agents of biological warfare so that he can blackmail world powers. Bond infiltrates Piz Gloria disguised as Sir Hilary Bray of the College of Arms. When his real identity is discovered, Bond escapes and reunites with Tracy, but she is captured by Blofeld after being caught in an avalanche.

The world powers refuse to attack Blofeld, so Draco leads the Unione Corse's attack on Piz Gloria and rescues Tracy. During the siege, Bond fights Blofeld on a bobsleigh run and believes Blofeld to be dead. Afterwards, Tracy and Bond marry, but Blofeld exacts his revenge when Tracy is killed in a hail of bullets destined for Bond.

Cast

JAMES BOND GEORGE LAZENBY
TRACY DIANA RIGG
BLOFELD TELLY SAVALAS
DRACO GABRIELE FERZETTI
IRMA BUNT ILSE STEPPAT
RUBY ANGELA SCOULAR
MONEYPENNY LOIS MAXWELL

Crew

DIRECTOR PETER HUNT
SCREENPLAY RICHARD MAIBAUM, JOHANNA M. HARWOOD, BERKELY MATHER
PRODUCERS HARRY SALTZMAN, ALBERT R. BROCCOLI
DIRECTOR OF PHOTOGRAPHY MICHAEL REED
TITLE SONG SUNG BY LOUIS ARMSTRONG

ALBERT R. BROCCOLI and HARRY SALTZMAN
present
JAMES BOND 007
in IAN FLEMING'S
"ON HER MAJESTY'S SECRET SERVICE"

starring GEORGE LAZENBY · DIANA RIGG · TELLY SAVALAS as Blofeld
also starring GABRIELE FERZETTI and ILSE STEPPAT Produced by ALBERT R. BROCCOLI and HARRY SALTZMAN
Directed by PETER HUNT · Screenplay by RICHARD MAIBAUM · Music by JOHN BARRY · PANAVISION® · TECHNICOLOR®

United Artists
Entertainment from Transamerica Corporation

COPYRIGHT © 1969 UNITED ARTISTS CORPORATION

A 70/9

1. In Maurice Binder's title sequence the clock and hourglass show that time is of the essence for Bond.

2. The teaser poster emphasizes the unknown quantity of a new Bond.

3. Bond (George Lazenby) rescues Tracy (Diana Rigg), who has tried to commit suicide by drowning.

4–5. After Bond pays for Tracy's gambling debt at the casino, she provokes him with his own gun, and then offers herself to him in lieu of payment.

"Everyone, particularly Peter Hunt, was impressed by George Lazenby. The infallible litmus test was to parade him in front of the office secretaries. Their eyes lit up as he swung past their desks and through our office."

—Cubby Broccoli

4

5

6. Filming Blofeld's patients playing curling at Piz Gloria while guards linger in the background. The 12 girls are being brainwashed by Blofeld to spread a virus that will sterilize the world's food supply.

7. Bond pretends to be Sir Hilary Bray of the London College of Arms, so that he can track down Ernst Stavro Blofeld (Telly Savalas).

8. Shooting began at Piz Gloria in Switzerland on October 21. Director of photography Michael Reed: "The first shot we did in the film was a crane shot bringing Lazenby up the stairs into the room where these 12 beautiful girls are."

"Director Peter Hunt was full of enthusiasm, and was very good with the actors. He had that unique ability to get the best out of everyone. Although people knock George Lazenby, from a film point of view* On Her Majesty's Secret Service *is a brilliant movie."

—John Glen, Second Unit Director and Editor

7

"I am catering for people's dreams."

—Harry Saltzman, Producer

8

9. His cover blown, Bond tries to escape from Blofeld. It was a very physical shoot for Lazenby, but he was up to the task.

10. Tracy and Bond are pursued around the track by Irma Bunt and Blofeld's henchmen. The sequence, directed by Anthony Squire, ends with a bang.

11. The numerous press stories about tension between Rigg and Lazenby did not affect their onscreen chemistry.

12. The tragic ending of the film, combined with the change in lead actor, contributed to the mixed reviews it received. However, the years have been kind, and it is now considered one of the best in the franchise.

"The odds were I'd get the part, because I wanted it more than anybody else."

—George Lazenby

Diamonds Are Forever

1971

RELEASE DATE December 14, 1971 (West Germany) | **RUNNING TIME** 120 minutes

Synopsis

MI6 assign Bond to investigate who is hoarding the world's supply of diamonds. The case leads Bond to Amsterdam, where he poses as criminal Peter Franks and meets Tiffany Case, a glamorous gemstone smuggler. Bond and Tiffany smuggle the diamonds to Las Vegas, where Bond suspects that reclusive industrialist Willard Whyte is behind the conspiracy.

Bond infiltrates Whyte's desert laboratory and finds that the diamonds are being used as part of a laser-beam satellite. Back in Vegas, Bond sneaks into Whyte's penthouse, where he comes face-to-face with his archnemesis, Blofeld, who has kidnapped Whyte and is impersonating him. Blofeld plans to hold the world hostage for ransom with the deadly satellite. After being left for dead by assassins Mr. Kidd and Mr. Wint, Bond and Tiffany follow Blofeld to his oil-rig base. As CIA helicopter gunships attack, Bond disarms the satellite and prevents Blofeld's escape. On the sea voyage back to London, Bond disposes of Kidd and Wint as they try to assassinate him.

Cast

JAMES BOND SEAN CONNERY
TIFFANY CASE JILL ST. JOHN
BLOFELD CHARLES GRAY
PLENTY O'TOOLE LANA WOOD
WILLARD WHYTE JIMMY DEAN
BERT SAXBY BRUCE CABOT
MR. KIDD PUTTER SMITH

Crew

DIRECTOR GUY HAMILTON
SCREENPLAY RICHARD MAIBAUM, TOM MANKIEWICZ
PRODUCERS HARRY SALTZMAN, ALBERT R. BROCCOLI
DIRECTOR OF PHOTOGRAPHY TED MOORE
TITLE SONG LYRICS DON BLACK
TITLE SONG SUNG BY SHIRLEY BASSEY

starring

JILL ST. JOHN

CHARLES GRAY

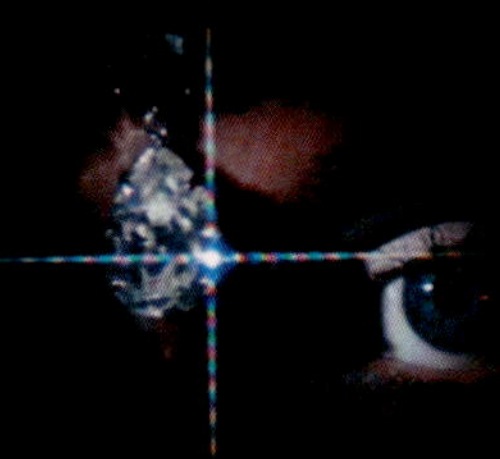

ALBERT R. BROCCOLI and HARRY SALTZMAN present
Sean Connery
as James Bond 007
in IAN FLEMING'S
"Diamonds Are Forever"
Forever
Forever
Forever
Forever
Forever
GP ALL AGES ADMITTED
THIS PICTURE CONTAINS MATERIAL WHICH MAY BE UNSUITABLE FOR PRE-TEENAGERS.
starring
JILL ST. JOHN as 'TIFFANY CASE' · CHARLES GRAY
also starring LANA WOOD as 'PLENTY O'TOOLE' · JIMMY DEAN · BRUCE CABOT · Produced by ALBERT R. BROCCOLI and HARRY SALTZMAN · Directed by GUY HAMILTON
Screenplay by RICHARD MAIBAUM and TOM MANKIEWICZ · Production Designed by KEN ADAM · Music by JOHN BARRY · PANAVISION® · TECHNICOLOR®
ORIGINAL MOTION PICTURE SCORE AVAILABLE ON UNITED ARTISTS RECORDS AND TAPES
United Artists
COPYRIGHT ©1971 UNITED ARTISTS CORPORATION

1. The title sequence by Maurice Binder.

2. The final poster by Robert McGinnis. The position of the diamonds raised eyebrows, although its apparent sexual connotations were accidental. The original layout had the two girls taller than Connery. At the last minute, United Artists's chief publicist, Don Smolen, had to alter the picture himself to make Connery taller: "If you look at it real carefully, he is the longest-waisted human being that anyone has ever seen."

"I think, if it ain't broke, don't fix it. Sean was just wonderful. He was James Bond to me."

—Jill St. John

3. The murder of Dr. Tynan (Henry Rowland, right) was shot in two ways: firstly with the scorpion placed in his mouth, as per the novel and script; then again with the creature being dropped down his back. "They thought that putting the scorpion in the mouth was too shocking," recalls Putter Smith (as Mr. Kidd, left). Bruce Glover (as Mr. Wint, middle), who held the scorpion, dealt with his fear by appealing to his ego: "Every actor wants attention, so I'm thinking, 'I'm the only guy on the set with a scorpion in my hand,' and boy, that's an attention grabber right there."

4. Bond (Sean Connery) attacks Peter Franks (Joe Robinson) in the climax of the lift fight.

5. When Bond is discovered at the Techtronics research center, he escapes across a fake lunar landscape.

"Stuntmen in general are wonderful to have around, because there's a certain joyousness, a danger—danger is an elixir of life."

—Bruce Glover

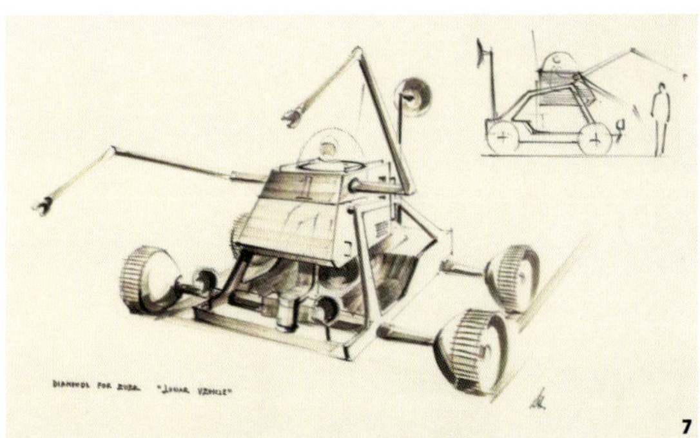

6. This stunt with a high-performance Ford Mustang Mach 1 turned into a continuity nightmare—this shot filmed at Universal City Studios did not match the shot filmed on location in Las Vegas.

7. Ken Adam's concept art for the moon buggy.

8. Mr. Kidd bursts into flames at the climax of *Diamonds Are Forever*. Stunt performer George Leech suffered burns to his wrists.

9. Deadly assassins Bambi (Lola Larson) and Thumper (Trina Parks) were originally envisioned as men. Guy Hamilton: "It would have been so easy to have Filipino servants and they karate kick him to death. Why not have two girls? I'd just seen the US tumbling team, and I was impressed with these girls doing flip-flops and things. I thought, 'I bet one of those girls flip-flopping would kick Bond before he knew what had hit him, and being a gentleman, he'd be rather surprised.' Give her a friend, and that's better than just Filipino heavies."

8

9

Live and Let Die

1973

RELEASE DATE June 27, 1973 (US) | **RUNNING TIME** 121 minutes

Synopsis

While investigating the deaths of three British agents, James Bond falls foul of gangster Mr. Big, who seems to have connections to Dr. Kananga, the president of San Monique. Bond follows leads to New Orleans, then to San Monique, where he is aided by double agent Rosie Carver. After freeing Kananga's girlfriend, Solitaire, a seer who foretells the future with Tarot cards, Bond discovers that Kananga and Mr. Big are one and the same. Via his chain of Fillet of Soul restaurants, Kananga plans to flood the USA with two tons of free heroin, which will put his competitors out of business and allow him to monopolize the drug's supply. When Solitaire is recaptured by Kananga, Bond, with help from CIA agent Felix Leiter and Quarrel Jr., returns to San Monique to kill Kananga and save Solitaire, before she is ritually sacrificed by Baron Samedi, the voodoo chief.

Cast

JAMES BOND ROGER MOORE
KANANGA/MR. BIG YAPHET KOTTO
SOLITAIRE JANE SEYMOUR
SHERIFF PEPPER CLIFTON JAMES
TEE HEE JULIUS W. HARRIS
BARON SAMEDI GEOFFREY HOLDER
LEITER DAVID HEDISON

Crew

DIRECTOR GUY HAMILTON
SCREENPLAY TOM MANKIEWICZ
PRODUCERS HARRY SALTZMAN, ALBERT R. BROCCOLI
DIRECTOR OF PHOTOGRAPHY TED MOORE
MUSIC GEORGE MARTIN
TITLE SONG SUNG BY PAUL MCCARTNEY AND WINGS

2

"We had to make Roger believe he was 007. He had to take on whole new dimensions, recognizing that Bond could be a mean bastard at times, a bit sadistic if the situation called for it, and that even his love scenes might need a touch of menace now and again."

—Cubby Broccoli

1. Main title backgrounds were shot on D Stage at Pinewood by Maurice Binder, including silhouetted naked girls, torches, skulls, and fronds of a fiberglass puffball changing color.

2. The UK release poster with art by Robert McGinnis.

3. Director Guy Hamilton (leaning on coffee-grinding machine) and M (Bernard Lee) in the kitchen of Bond's Mews Flat. After *Dr. No,* this was only the second time we have seen Bond's home.

4. Tuesday, March 6, 1973. 5th Avenue, between 117th and 118th Streets, Harlem, New York City: Stuntmen Franklin Scott and Teddy Thompson play two hoods aiming to kill Bond (Roger Moore) on Mr. Big's orders.

"Roger is not Sean, and vice versa. You've got to forget whatever images you have in your mind."

—Guy Hamilton, Director

5. Bond's roofless "San Monique Transport" bus sits on the dock at Hampton Wharf Jetty, Falmouth, Jamaica, so 007 can escape with Solitaire on Quarrel Jr.'s boat, the *Cutty Sark*. Moore, seated on the top deck, on Sunday, December 10, 1972.

6. Dr. Kananga (Yaphet Kotto) and his seer Solitaire, aka Simone Latrelle (Jane Seymour), who has "the power of the Obeah," in Solitaire's throne room.

7. Bond's GT-150 jumps Highway 39 in a stunt performed by Jerry Comeaux. It was filmed on October 15, 1972, day three of the shoot.

EVINRUDE
10
SHERIFF'S
DEPARTMENT

8. Solitaire is menaced by Dambala (Michael Ebbin) and a nonvenomous Emerald Tree Boa at the voodoo cemetery at Pinewood, early February 1973.

9. Concept designs of the lair, supervised by Syd Cain.

"I wanted my movements to be more Haitian, holding the knife in that downward kind of position. So Kananga held the knife in a very unusual kind of way."

—Yaphet Kotto

10. The American influence: Bond does not brandish a Walther PPK, but a Smith & Wesson Magnum, to rescue Solitaire. Though there was a great deal of pressure on him, Moore settled quickly into the role, showing the effortless élan that would become his signature.

11. His bonds cut by his buzz-saw Rolex, Bond fights Kananga to the death.

10

11

The Man with the Golden Gun

1974

RELEASE DATE December 19, 1974 (UK and US) | **RUNNING TIME** 125 minutes

Synopsis
James Bond receives a gold bullet inscribed with "007," signifying he has been targeted by high-class professional assassin Francisco Scaramanga, known as "The Man with the Golden Gun." 007 is relieved of his current assignment, the search for scientist Gibson and his solex agitator, the solution to the global energy crisis, and determines to find Scaramanga. The trail leads to specialist armorer Lazar in Macau, then to Scaramanga's contact Andrea and industrialist Hai Fat in Hong Kong. After killing Gibson, Scaramanga steals the solex agitator and kidnaps MI6 liaison officer Mary Goodnight. A homing device leads Bond to Scaramanga's lair, an isolated island in Chinese waters. Bond travels there by seaplane, kills Scaramanga in a duel, retrieves the solex agitator, and escapes with Goodnight in Scaramanga's junk.

Cast
JAMES BOND ROGER MOORE
SCARAMANGA CHRISTOPHER LEE
GOODNIGHT BRITT EKLAND
ANDREA MAUD ADAMS
NICK NACK HERVÉ VILLECHAIZE
SHERIFF J.W. PEPPER CLIFTON JAMES
HAI FAT RICHARD LOO

Crew
DIRECTOR GUY HAMILTON
SCREENPLAY TOM MANKIEWICZ, RICHARD MAIBAUM
PRODUCERS HARRY SALTZMAN, ALBERT R. BROCCOLI
DIRECTORS OF PHOTOGRAPHY TED MOORE, OSWALD MORRIS
PRODUCTION DESIGN PETER MURTON
TITLE SONG SUNG BY LULU

THE WORLD'S GREATEST VILLAINS
TRIED TO KILL JAMES BOND

DR. NO.
He couldn't kill Bond with a cyanide cigarette and the world's largest tarantula.

ROSA KLEB.
She couldn't kill Bond with an assassin trained from birth.

GOLDFINGER AND ODD JOB.
They couldn't split Bond in half with a laser beam or with the world's deadliest hat.

BLOFELD.
He tried to kill Bond with a deadly virus and ten of the most beautiful women in the world.

NOW IT'S
SCARAMANGA'S
TURN TO TRY

ALBERT R. BROCCOLI and HARRY SALTZMAN present

ROGER MOORE
AS
JAMES BOND
007

in IAN FLEMING'S

"THE MAN WITH THE GOLDEN GUN"

with CHRISTOPHER LEE · BRITT EKLAND · Produced by ALBERT R. BROCCOLI and HARRY SALTZMAN
Directed by GUY HAMILTON · Screenplay by RICHARD MAIBAUM and TOM MANKIEWICZ · Music by JOHN BARRY

PG PARENTAL GUIDANCE SUGGESTED SOME MATERIAL MAY NOT BE SUITABLE FOR PRE-TEENAGERS

ORIGINAL MOTION PICTURE SOUNDTRACK AVAILABLE ON UNITED ARTISTS UA RECORDS AND TAPES

·COLOR·

United Artists
Entertainment from Transamerica Corporation

1. The title sequence. Harry Saltzman's assistant Sue St. John: "Maurice Binder always had a hard time getting titles on time. He wasn't a procrastinator, he just liked working to a heavy deadline and sometimes he'd miss the deadline. But everybody knew he'd come through in the end so nobody really got cross with him."

2. US poster, Advance Style B, by Robert McGinnis, featuring previous Bond nemeses Dr. No, Rosa Klebb, Grant, Goldfinger, Oddjob, and Blofeld.

3. The Astor-Spiral 360 jump, on June 1, 1974, at Klong Rangsit.

4. Scaramanga (Christopher Lee) shows Bond how he can harness the power of the sun; he uses his "golden gun" to destroy the seaplane.

6

***“It’s always struck me that Bond is rather like* The Perils of Pauline.**
It’s laughs, it’s excitement, suspense, pretty girls, adventure, all the things that movies were all about when I was a kid.”

—Guy Hamilton

5. An effigy of Bond, its fingers used for target practice by Scaramanga, in the villain’s shooting gallery.

6. Fight to the death: Scaramanga and Bond, the best in their respective fields, on the beach at Khao Phing Kan Island, near Phuket. Bond’s Walther has a six-shot magazine, while Scaramanga’s 4.2mm golden pistol is single-shot.

7. James Bond: “Good night, sir!” James and Mary Goodnight (Britt Ekland) make their escape in Scaramanga’s junk.

The Spy Who Loved Me

1977

RELEASE DATE July 7, 1977 (UK) | **RUNNING TIME** 120 minutes

Synopsis

After British and Russian submarines carrying nuclear warheads vanish, James Bond travels to Egypt, where illicit microfilm plans for a submarine tracking system are being offered for sale. In Cairo he meets KGB agent Major Anya Amasova, who is on the same mission. After their contact is murdered, they fight Jaws, a steel-toothed villain in the pay of industrialist Karl Stromberg.

MI6 and the KGB order Bond and Amasova to work together. In Sardinia, they encounter Stromberg and suspect that he is behind the submarine disappearances. After being chased by Jaws and Stromberg's henchmen, they escape underwater in Bond's amphibious Lotus Esprit.

Onboard a US submarine, the spies learn more about Stromberg's underwater base, Atlantis, and about his supertanker, the *Liparus*. When their sub is captured by the *Liparus*, a huge vessel that "swallows" submarines, Bond discovers Stromberg's plan to trigger a nuclear war. Bond leads the captured sailors against the *Liparus's* crew and defeats Stromberg. Atlantis sinks but Jaws escapes.

Cast

JAMES BOND ROGER MOORE
MAJOR ANYA AMASOVA/AGENT TRIPLE X BARBARA BACH
KARL STROMBERG CURT JURGENS
JAWS RICHARD KIEL
NAOMI CAROLINE MUNRO
GENERAL ANATOL GOGOL WALTER GOTELL
SIR FREDERICK GRAY GEOFFREY KEEN

Crew

DIRECTOR LEWIS GILBERT
SCREENPLAY CHRISTOPHER WOOD, RICHARD MAIBAUM
PRODUCER ALBERT R. BROCCOLI
DIRECTOR OF PHOTOGRAPHY CLAUDE RENOIR
TITLE SONG SUNG BY CARLY SIMON

IT'S THE BIGGEST. IT'S THE BEST. IT'S BOND. AND BEYOND.

3

1. Maurice Binder's title sequence.

2. Early concept art for *The Spy Who Loved Me* poster by Bob Peak.

3. Derek Meddings and his modelers put an incredible amount of detail into the Atlantis model.

4–5. Ken Adam flew out to Japan to visit the Aquapolis exhibit at Expo '75 but was disappointed by its design. "It looked like a giant oil rig." His sketches made Atlantis more fantastical, with a curved design and spider-like legs.

6. Derek Meddings and his team took the Atlantis models out to the Bahamas. Here, Lamar Boren films the Atlantis submerging and Michael G. Wilson is in the foreground with the yellow-tipped snorkel. Derek Meddings: "We had these enormous structures which we'd put on the seabed. It was like an enormous four-poster bed with all these rams and things in there so that we can actually pull Atlantis down under the water and create all this white water bubbling up. I thought it was quite a good shot."

"My designs had always been very linear and I wanted to work with more curved shapes. So the design of Atlantis, which looked like some kind of spider coming out of the water, was all domed and curved surfaces."

—Ken Adam

7. Bond and Anya (Barbara Bach) search for Jaws (Richard Kiel) among the pillars of the Great Hypostyle Hall in the Karnak Temple Complex, unaware that Jaws is spying on them from above.

8. Russian agent Major Anya Amasova and British special agent James Bond reluctantly join forces to locate plans for a submarine tracking system.

9. Bond improvises and turns a light fitting into an electric toothbrush during the fight with Jaws onboard the train to Sardinia.

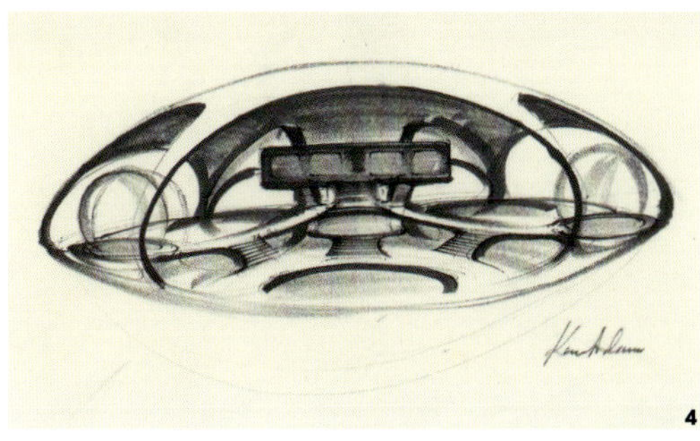

4

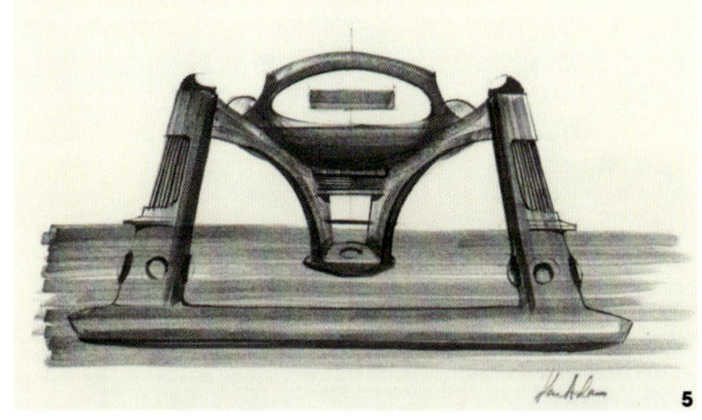

5

6

7

8

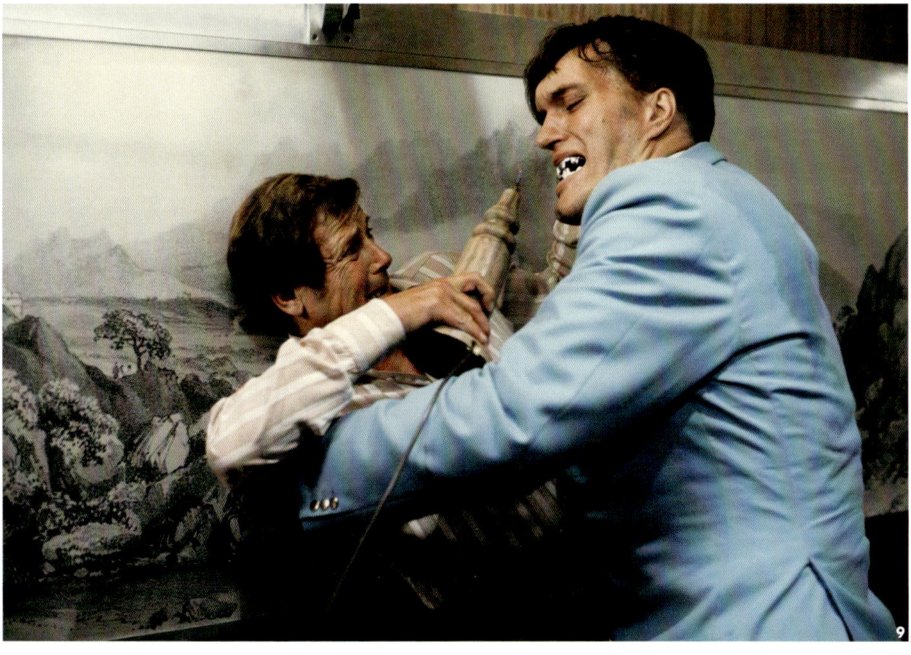

9

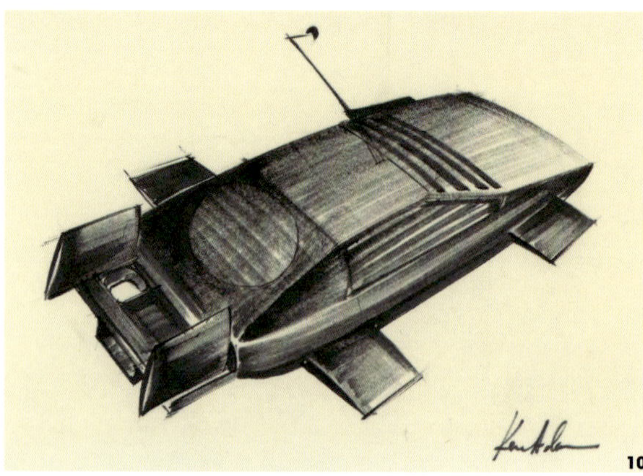

10. Ken Adam drew the concept sketches for the submarine car: "The Lotus Esprit lent itself beautifully, with that very streamlined body, to work as a submarine."

11. The Lotus is driven into the sea during the chase and transforms into a submarine. This shot was achieved by shooting the empty shell of a Lotus off the end of an air cannon.

"Ken is one of the great set designers of all time. But everything gets blown up in Bond, which is rather sad."

—Roger Moore

11

12. Adam's *Liparus* set inaugurated the 007 Stage at Pinewood. Stromberg's supertanker was supposed to be big enough to hold several submarines.

Paul Weston: "It was magnificent. It had hundreds of extras running around and dozens and dozens of stuntmen."

13. An early concept sketch by Ken Adam for the docking bay inside the *Liparus*.

13

Moonraker

1979

RELEASE DATE June 26, 1979 (UK) | **RUNNING TIME** 126 minutes

Synopsis

When the *Moonraker* space shuttle is hijacked, M sends Bond to the shuttle's manufacturer, Hugo Drax, to investigate. Bond follows clues that lead him first to Venice, where he discovers Drax's laboratory manufacturing a highly toxic nerve gas, and then to Rio, where he teams up with CIA agent and astrophysicist Dr. Holly Goodhead. At every turn they are attacked by Jaws on Drax's orders. Bond goes into the jungle to find the source of the nerve gas, but instead discovers that Drax is launching multiple space shuttles filled with couples who will find safe haven in his secret space station. Drax plans to send pods containing deadly nerve gas to Earth to destroy the human race, and will later repopulate it with his master race of perfect physical specimens.

A platoon of US marines arrive in a shuttle and defeat Drax's men in a laser battle, while Bond and Dr. Goodhead track and destroy the deadly gas.

Cast

JAMES BOND ROGER MOORE
DR. HOLLY GOODHEAD LOIS CHILES
HUGO DRAX MICHAEL LONSDALE
JAWS RICHARD KIEL
CORINNE DUFOUR CORINNE CLÉRY
M BERNARD LEE
Q DESMOND LLEWELYN

Crew

DIRECTOR LEWIS GILBERT
SCREENPLAY CHRISTOPHER WOOD
PRODUCER ALBERT R. BROCCOLI
DIRECTOR OF PHOTOGRAPHY JEAN TOURNIER
PRODUCTION DESIGNER KEN ADAM
TITLE SONG SUNG BY SHIRLEY BASSEY

Albert R. Broccoli
presents
ROGER MOORE
as
JAMES BOND 007
in Ian Fleming's
MOONRAKER
J. BOND
007
Co-starring Lois Chiles Richard Kiel as 'Jaws' Michael Lonsdale as 'Drax' and Corinne Clery
Produced by Albert R. Broccoli Directed by Lewis Gilbert Screenplay by Christopher Wood
Music by John Barry Lyrics by Hal David Production Design by Ken Adam Executive Producer Michael G. Wilson
ORIGINAL MOTION PICTURE SOUNDTRACK ON UNITED ARTISTS RECORDS AND TAPES
Associate Producer William P. Cartlidge Filmed in Panavision®
DOLBY STEREO™
Title Song Performed by Shirley Bassey
United Artists
A Transamerica Company
Copyright © 1979 United Artists Corporation. All rights reserved.

3

1. Maurice Binder mixes the elements of the Earth, orchids, and perfect people to create the title sequence.

2. Artist Dan Goozee used photo references to create the Moonraker poster campaign. Note that in the artwork James Bond is wearing a tuxedo under his spacesuit.

3. Bond (doubled by Dickie Graydon) almost falls off the top of the cable car when Jaws stops it in midair from below.

4. Corinne Cléry and Roger Moore share a joke on set, watched by director Lewis Gilbert in the foreground. Roger Moore: "I must apologize to all the people that I ever worked with. I make jokes right up until the last minute."

5. Hugo Drax (Michael Lonsdale, seated) plans to destroy all life on Earth using a toxin developed from a rare Amazonian orchid (in glass bubble), and then later repopulate the planet with his "Master Race" of genetically perfect people. Mercenary assassin Jaws (Richard Kiel, right) attempts to kill Bond, who is investigating Drax.

6. The interior of the Command Satellite, as designed by Ken Adam, consisted of multiple levels, which made it very difficult to film.

"The most expensive thing in the world is Ken Adam with a blank piece of paper and a charcoal pencil."

—William Cartlidge, Associate Producer

4

"When you do a Bond film, you don't just get a producer, you get a family. And what's wonderful is that they make you feel part of that family."

—Lewis Gilbert, Director

5

For Your Eyes Only

1981

RELEASE DATE June 24, 1981 (UK) | **RUNNING TIME** 127 minutes

Synopsis

James Bond is ordered to retrieve the Automatic Targeting Attack Communicator (ATAC), housed on a sunken spy ship, the *St. Georges*. When Sir Timothy Havelock, a marine archeologist secretly helping the British to locate the ship, is murdered along with his wife, Bond is dispatched to Spain to find out who hired the hit man, Gonzales, but before he can find out, Gonzales is killed by Havelock's daughter, Melina. In Italy, Bond and Melina seek organized-crime figure Milos Columbo through businessman Aristotle Kristatos, then travel to Corfu to pursue Columbo.

Columbo reveals that Kristatos is responsible for the Havelocks' murder and is working with the Russians to obtain the ATAC. After retrieving the ATAC from the wreck of the *St. Georges*, Bond and Melina are captured by Kristatos, but survive his attempt to drown them.

Aided by Columbo, Bond and Melina infiltrate the mountaintop monastery of St. Cyril's, where Bond retrieves the ATAC and prevents Melina from killing Kristatos, who dies by Columbo's hand. As the Russians arrive to collect the ATAC, Bond destroys it, so neither East nor West can have it.

Cast

JAMES BOND ROGER MOORE
MELINA HAVELOCK CAROLE BOUQUET
ARISTOTLE KRISTATOS JULIAN GLOVER
MILOS COLUMBO TOPOL
BIBI DAHL LYNN-HOLLY JOHNSON
COUNTESS LISL CASSANDRA HARRIS
LOCQUE MICHAEL GOTHARD

Crew

DIRECTOR JOHN GLEN
SCREENPLAY RICHARD MAIBAUM, MICHAEL G. WILSON
PRODUCER ALBERT R. BROCCOLI
DIRECTOR OF PHOTOGRAPHY ALAN HUME
TITLE SONG SUNG BY SHEENA EASTON

3

1. For the first time in the series' near 20-year history, Maurice Binder's title sequence featured the singer of the film's song. Sheena Easton's participation made it akin to a promotional video.

2. Concept artwork for the *For Your Eyes Only* poster. Hy Smith, head of publicity for United Artists, hired Bill Gold to create the controversial poster.

3. Bond watches as Locque's Mercedes plunges over the cliff. The final scene gives the film a striking moment of ruthlessness worthy of Fleming.

4. Roger Moore, tied to Carole Bouquet, sharing a laugh before shooting a close-up for the keel-hauling sequence.

5. Filming the keel-hauling sequence in the Bahamas, where Bond and Melina are dragged through razor-sharp coral—and shark-infested waters—by Kristatos's boat.

6. With the monks putting out laundry and flags (right) to make filming difficult, Peter Lamont built a partial set on the adjoining rock (left), allowing for the final sequences to progress unhindered.

7. Filming the finale, where Melina (Carole Bouquet) finds herself with the opportunity to take her revenge on Kristatos (Julian Glover, right) for murdering her parents, but is talked out of it by Bond.

Octopussy

1983

RELEASE DATE June 6, 1983 (UK) | **RUNNING TIME** 131 minutes

Synopsis

009 is found dead at the British Ambassador's residence in East Berlin, dressed as a circus clown and carrying a fake Fabergé egg. MI6 sends Bond to investigate when the real egg appears at a London auction. Bond swaps the real egg with the fake, and drives up the bidding against exiled Afghan prince Kamal Khan, who ultimately wins the auction.

Bond follows Khan back to his palace in Rajasthan, India, where he discovers that Khan is working with Orlov, a renegade Soviet general, and is using Octopussy's circus troupe to smuggle Soviet treasures into the West. Bond infiltrates the circus, and finds that Orlov has replaced the treasures with a nuclear warhead, primed to explode during the show at a US Air Force base in West Germany. He convinces Octopussy that Khan has betrayed her and she assists Bond in deactivating the warhead.

Bond and Octopussy return to India and launch an assault on Khan's palace. Khan and bodyguard Gobinda capture Octopussy as they escape in an airplane. Bond clings to the fuselage in a fight to the death with Gobinda, and manages to rescue Octopussy moments before the plane crashes, killing Khan.

Cast

JAMES BOND ROGER MOORE
OCTOPUSSY MAUD ADAMS
KAMAL KHAN LOUIS JOURDAN
GOBINDA KABIR BEDI
GENERAL ORLOV STEVEN BERKOFF
MAGDA KRISTINA WAYBORN
VIJAY VIJAY AMRITRAJ

Crew

DIRECTOR JOHN GLEN
SCREENPLAY RICHARD MAIBAUM, MICHAEL G. WILSON
PRODUCER ALBERT R. BROCCOLI
DIRECTOR OF PHOTOGRAPHY ALAN HUME
TITLE SONG SUNG BY RITA COOLIDGE

James Bond's
all time high.
ALBERT R. BROCCOLI
presents
ROGER MOORE
as IAN FLEMING'S
JAMES BOND 007
in
OCTOPUSSY
Starring
MAUD ADAMS, LOUIS JOURDAN, KRISTINA WAYBORN, KABIR BEDI
Produced by
ALBERT R. BROCCOLI
Directed by
JOHN GLEN
Screen Story and Screenplay by GEORGE MacDONALD FRASER and RICHARD MAIBAUM & MICHAEL G. WILSON
Theme song performed by
RITA COOLIDGE
Executive Producer
MICHAEL G. WILSON
Production Designer
PETER LAMONT
Associate Producer
TOM PEVSNER
Music by
JOHN BARRY
PG PARENTAL GUIDANCE SUGGESTED
SOME MATERIAL MAY NOT BE SUITABLE FOR CHILDREN
SOUNDTRACK AVAILABLE ON A&M RECORDS AND TAPES
© 1983 DANJAQ S.A. ALL RIGHTS RESERVED
DISTRIBUTED BY
MGM/UA
ENTERTAINMENT CO.

1. Maurice Binder's title sequence for *Octopussy*, with its striking use of laser beams.

2. *Octopussy's* poster art, painted by Renato Casaro.

3. James Bond goes Tarzan while filming the tiger-hunt sequence in Udaipur.

4. Filming the taxi-chase sequence in Udaipur, September 1982. Stunt driver Rémy Julienne suitably souped up the three-wheeled taxis to have them be able to perform their Bond requirements.

5. The landing bed for the taxi jump, an unfamiliar sight in densely populated Udaipur, which inevitably led to a gathering of hundreds of curious passersby.

6. Octopussy (Maud Adams) and Kamal Khan (Louis Jourdan) discuss their plans, while she feeds her signature pet.

7. Filming the climactic fight sequence between Gobinda and Bond in Utah, June 1982. Stuntmen Jake Lombard and B.J. Worth doubled for Bond and Gobinda for three weeks to complete the scene.

VN75WB

Never Say Never Again

1983

RELEASE DATE October 6, 1983 (US) | **RUNNING TIME** 134 minutes

Synopsis

Communications officer Jack Petachi helps SPECTRE steal two cruise missiles and is then killed by Fatima Blush. As SPECTRE holds NATO to ransom, Bond follows the only clue—a matchbook with a flag design—to billionaire Maximilian Largo in Nassau. From there, Bond follows Largo to Nice, begins flirting with Domino Petachi, Largo's mistress, and dispatches assassin Fatima Blush. Teaming up with CIA agent Felix Leiter, Bond boards Largo's ship, *The Flying Saucer*, where he is captured, but manages to enlist the help of Domino when she finds out that Largo was responsible for her brother Jack's death.

At Palmyra, Largo's North African retreat, Bond and Domino escape, and then Bond tracks the missing missile to an underground cavern. In the final underwater confrontation, as Bond is diffusing the warhead, Domino saves Bond's life by killing Largo with a harpoon, gaining revenge for the murder of her brother.

Cast

JAMES BOND SEAN CONNERY
DOMINO PETACHI KIM BASINGER
MAXIMILIAN LARGO KLAUS MARIA BRANDAUER
FATIMA BLUSH BARBARA CARRERA
ERNST STAVRO BLOFELD MAX VON SYDOW
FELIX LEITER BERNIE CASEY
Q / ALGY THE ARMORER ALEC MCCOWEN

Crew

DIRECTOR IRVIN KERSHNER
SCREENPLAY LORENZO SEMPLE JR.
PRODUCER JACK SCHWARTZMAN
DIRECTOR OF PHOTOGRAPHY
DOUGLAS SLOCOMBE

SEAN CONNERY

is JAMES BOND in

NEVER SAY NEVER AGAIN

JACK SCHWARTZMAN and KEVIN McCLORY Present
A TALIAFILM Production An IRVIN KERSHNER Film

SEAN CONNERY

"NEVER SAY NEVER AGAIN"

Also starring
KLAUS MARIA BRANDAUER · MAX VON SYDOW · BARBARA CARRERA · KIM BASINGER · BERNIE CASEY · ALEC McCOWEN and EDWARD FOX as "M"
Director of Photography DOUGLAS SLOCOMBE B.S.C. Music by MICHEL LEGRAND Executive Producer KEVIN McCLORY Screenplay by LORENZO SEMPLE, JR.
Based on an Original Story by KEVIN McCLORY, JACK WHITTINGHAM and IAN FLEMING Directed by IRVIN KERSHNER Produced by JACK SCHWARTZMAN
Title song sung by LANI HALL Music by MICHEL LEGRAND Lyrics by ALAN and MARILYN BERGMAN

PG PARENTAL GUIDANCE SUGGESTED
SOME MATERIAL MAY NOT BE SUITABLE FOR CHILDREN

DOLBY STEREO
IN SELECTED THEATRES

Panavision® Technicolor®

DISTRIBUTED BY WARNER BROS
A WARNER COMMUNICATIONS COMPANY

1. Sean Connery returned to the role of James Bond after a break of 12 years, but only on the condition that he had approval of director, cast, and script.

2. The poster for *Never Say Never Again*. The film premiered on October 6, 1983, and grossed $160 million worldwide.

3. Originally cut together with a ticking clock on the soundtrack, which added tension, a song was added in the final cut that dissipated any inherent tension in the scene.

4

4. As Bond unties the hostage (Wendy Leech), she stabs him. It is only then that we realize this is a training exercise. Lorenzo Semple Jr. wrote the first-draft screenplay: "The major change we made from the novel was that James Bond was in semi-retirement, and must force his way back into the action. He's the last person M wants involved, because he's too dangerous and they don't do things that way any more."

5

5. Much of the fight scene with Lippe (Pat Roach) was improvised on location with stunt coordinator Vic Armstrong.

6. Fatima (Barbara Carrera) seduces Bond. Barbara Carrera: "She sees herself as Kali, the Hindu goddess of death and destruction, and I see her as a black widow spider. Before she kills her prey she must make love to him!"

"Fatima is like a bad child who does not see the evil in what she is doing. She just enjoys doing it."

—Barbara Carrera

6

7

"It's important to use the humanity of the character as a base because however original the gadgets are, James Bond still has to figure his way out!"

—Sean Connery

7. Bond rescues Domino (Kim Basinger) from Palmyra, Largo's base in North Africa. Director Irvin Kershner: "Bond does what we would love to be able to do. He displays the courage we would all love to have. He fights against terrible odds. To wipe away evil with one bullet is a fantasy."

8. Largo (Klaus Maria Brandauer) has stolen two cruise missiles and SPECTRE is using them to hold the world to ransom. Bond follows Largo as he places one of the warheads underground to destroy the oil fields of Saudi Arabia. Here Bond tries to dislodge a statue and crush the warhead before it is armed.

9. Bond vows "Never again" and kisses Domino.

"Sean was sensitive, masculine, he had a glint in his eye, and had a great voice. What else do you need to play Bond?"

—Irvin Kershner, Director

9

A View to a Kill

1985

RELEASE DATE May 22, 1985 (US) | **RUNNING TIME** 126 minutes

Synopsis

A microchip James Bond recovers from the corpse of 003 in Siberia is a copy of one that is impervious to the magnetic pulse of a nuclear blast. It is made by a company recently acquired by Anglo-French combine Zorin Industries, so Bond is assigned to investigate Max Zorin.

In Paris, Bond meets detective Aubergine to find out about Zorin, but Aubergine is killed by Zorin's bodyguard, May Day. Bond poses as a horse trainer to infiltrate Zorin's equestrian estate, but his cover is blown and Zorin tries to drown him. 007 survives and tracks Zorin to San Francisco, where Zorin is planning Project Main Strike: the destruction of Silicon Valley by detonating explosions in mines beneath lakes and flooding the Hayward and San Andreas faults. With help from geologist Stacey Sutton, Bond sabotages Zorin's scheme. Finding an unexpected ally in May Day, whom Zorin has betrayed, Bond prevents the main explosion from detonating. As Zorin escapes in his airship, he kidnaps Stacey. The final confrontation between Bond and Zorin is atop the Golden Gate Bridge in San Francisco Bay, where Zorin falls to his death.

Cast

JAMES BOND ROGER MOORE
MAX ZORIN CHRISTOPHER WALKEN
STACEY SUTTON TANYA ROBERTS
MAY DAY GRACE JONES
SIR GODFREY TIBBETT PATRICK MACNEE
SCARPINE PATRICK BAUCHAU
CHUCK LEE DAVID YIP

Crew

DIRECTOR JOHN GLEN
SCREENPLAY RICHARD MAIBAUM, MICHAEL G. WILSON
PRODUCERS ALBERT R. BROCCOLI, MICHAEL G. WILSON
DIRECTOR OF PHOTOGRAPHY ALAN HUME
TITLE SONG SUNG BY DURAN DURAN

HAS JAMES BOND FINALLY
MET HIS MATCH?
ALBERT R. BROCCOLI Presents
ROGER MOORE
as IAN FLEMING'S
JAMES BOND 007
A VIEW TO A KILL
Starring TANYA ROBERTS · GRACE JONES · PATRICK MACNEE
and CHRISTOPHER WALKEN Music by JOHN BARRY Production Designer PETER LAMONT
Associate Producer TOM PEVSNER Produced by ALBERT R. BROCCOLI and MICHAEL G. WILSON
Directed by JOHN GLEN Screenplay by RICHARD MAIBAUM and MICHAEL G. WILSON
PG PARENTAL GUIDANCE SUGGESTED
SOME MATERIAL MAY NOT BE SUITABLE FOR CHILDREN
ORIGINAL MOTION PICTURE SOUNDTRACK
ON CAPITOL RECORDS AND CASSETTES
Title Song Performed by
DURAN DURAN
TECHNICOLOR®
Prints in METROCOLOR®
PANAVISION®
DOLBY STEREO

1. One hundred and sixteen girls were auditioned to appear in the titles, and 12 were selected. The luminous visual effects were achieved with ultraviolet paint. The titles also featured freestyle skiers Mike Nemesvary and Julia Snell from the British Ski Foundation, with Nemesvary performing trampoline flips on skis.

2. US poster artwork by Daniel J. Goozee.

3. Filming Roger Moore on the Eiffel Tower staircase. The production had use of the tower from 7:00 a.m. to 10:00 a.m. before the lifts were opened up to the public.

4. Topless and backless, the Renault, driven by stunt double Martin Grace, swerves towards stunt pedestrians in Paris.

5. Bond hangs off the ladder of the speeding fire truck.

6. Avenger and Saint: Patrick Macnee and Moore, with Cubby's Silver Cloud, share a joke at Chantilly. Previously, they had been teamed as Sherlock Holmes and Dr. Watson in the TV movie *Sherlock Holmes in New York* (1976).

5

"Nowadays you'd put a lot of the stunts and effects in digitally, but in those days we did everything for real."

—Anthony Waye, Production Supervisor

6

"I think of Grace Jones more as a performance artist than anything else. She's done a lot of wonderful, strange, and edgy types of modeling, and she turned out to be a great character."

—Michael G. Wilson

7. Grace Jones and Christopher Walken rehearsed their karate sequence at Pineapple Dance Studio, London, with stunt arranger Doug Robinson, before filming it in the pool room, as Zorin's gymnasium, at Pinewood.

8. Max Zorin (Christopher Walken) mows down his own miners with an Uzi, the weapon of choice for 1980s screen villains.

9. The third-scale miniature of the Main Strike mine is flooded as part of the finale of Zorin's Project Main Strike, early February 1985.

8

9

The Living Daylights

1987

RELEASE DATE June 29, 1987 (UK) | **RUNNING TIME** 130 minutes

Synopsis
After a training exercise in Gibraltar is hijacked and an MI6 agent is murdered, it seems that the KGB's old policy of *Smert Spionam* (Death to Spies) has been reactivated. Bond is sent to Czechoslovakia to support the defection of a Russian Army Officer, Koskov. He becomes suspicious when the sniper he has to assassinate appears to be a glamorous cellist, Kara Milovy. Later, when Koskov is kidnapped from the MI6 safe house, Bond's suspicions are heightened and he combines his official assignment to assassinate General Leonid Pushkin—the new head of the KGB, whom Koskov has named as the initiator of the *Smert Spionam* policy—with an investigation into Kara and Koskov. Bond, with Kara in tow, pursues Koskov to Tangier, where he is hiding with arms/drug dealer Whitaker and his hired killer, Necros. Betrayed by Kara, Bond is kidnapped and taken to Afghanistan. He escapes and, with the assistance of an army of Afghan rebels led by the charismatic Kamran Shah, brings down Whitaker's illegal activities.

Cast
JAMES BOND TIMOTHY DALTON
KARA MILOVY MARYAM D'ABO
GENERAL GEORGI KOSKOV JEROEN KRABBÉ
BRAD WHITAKER JOE DON BAKER
GENERAL LEONID PUSHKIN JOHN RHYS-DAVIES
KAMRAN SHAH ART MALIK
NECROS ANDREAS WISNIEWSKI

Crew
DIRECTOR JOHN GLEN
SCREENPLAY MICHAEL G. WILSON, RICHARD MAIBAUM
PRODUCERS ALBERT R. BROCCOLI, MICHAEL G. WILSON
DIRECTOR OF PHOTOGRAPHY ALEC MILLS
TITLE SONG SUNG BY A-HA

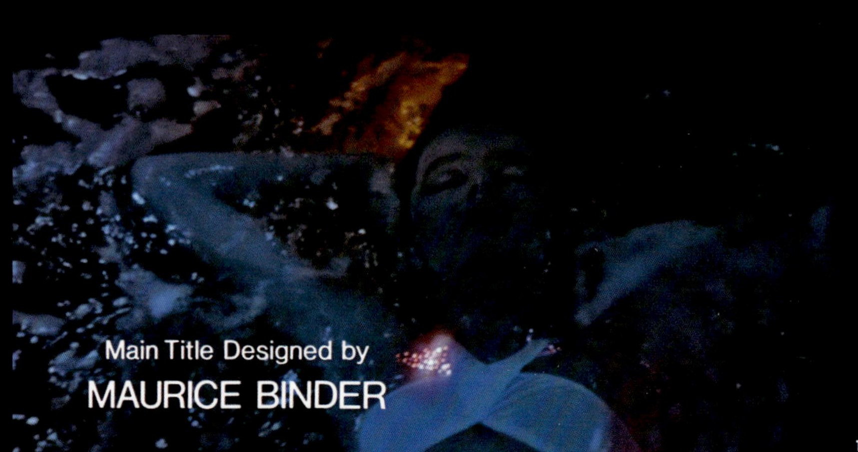

2

"With Bond, I wanted to capture that occasional sense of vulnerability. He remains very much a man, but is a tarnished man—he's not perfect."

—Timothy Dalton

> **"The Living Daylights *introduced another fascinating actress to the Bond scene, Maryam d'Abo. Her love scene with Timothy achieved the maturer level we were aiming at in Bond's amorous relationships."***
>
> —Cubby Broccoli

1. Title sequence designed by Maurice Binder.

2. Poster for *The Living Daylights.*

3. In Vienna, Bond (Timothy Dalton) discovers the body of MI6 ally Saunders, the latest victim of the KGB's policy to kill all foreign spies.

4. James Bond resting during the shooting of the magic-carpet stunt in Tangier on November 5, 1986. This stunt was part of the post-Pushkin "assassination" chase, but was later cut.

5. Bond and Kara (Maryam d'Abo) make love while hiding out in Kamran Shah's abode.

6. On location in Morocco, Bond flies a Hercules C-130, dropping a bomb on the bridge to prevent the Russians from following the rebels.

7. Back at Pinewood, a model of the bridge is bombed and explodes.

"The Bond movies are a special-effects man's dream, because you've got big explosions, you've got massive mechanical hydraulic rigs, you've got teensy-weensy gadgets, and you've got exotic places to go to."

—Chris Corbould, Special Effects

8. At Pinewood Studios, Timothy Dalton and Andreas Wisniewski film close-ups of the fight to the death on the nets hanging from the back of the plane.

9. John Barry conducting the orchestra as Kara makes her debut in the West. Filmed in Vienna on October 15, 1986.

Licence to Kill

1989

RELEASE DATE June 13, 1989 (UK) | **RUNNING TIME** 132 minutes

Synopsis
En route to the wedding of his friend Felix Leiter in Florida, Bond and Leiter take a detour to arrest drug baron Franz Sanchez. It doesn't take long, however, for Sanchez to break himself out of jail, and kill the new Mrs. Leiter and maim Felix. Bond seeks revenge. With his license revoked by the British government, and with the aid of CIA operative Pam Bouvier as well as MI6 gadget specialist Q, they plan to bring Sanchez and his entire corrupt drug empire to its knees.

Cast
JAMES BOND TIMOTHY DALTON
PAM BOUVIER CAREY LOWELL
FRANZ SANCHEZ ROBERT DAVI
LUPE LAMORA TALISA SOTO
MILTON KREST ANTHONY ZERBE
SHARKEY FRANK MCRAE
JOE BUTCHER WAYNE NEWTON

Crew
DIRECTOR JOHN GLEN
SCREENPLAY MICHAEL G. WILSON, RICHARD MAIBAUM
PRODUCERS ALBERT R. BROCCOLI, MICHAEL G. WILSON
DIRECTOR OF PHOTOGRAPHY ALEC MILLS
TITLE SONG SUNG BY GLADYS KNIGHT

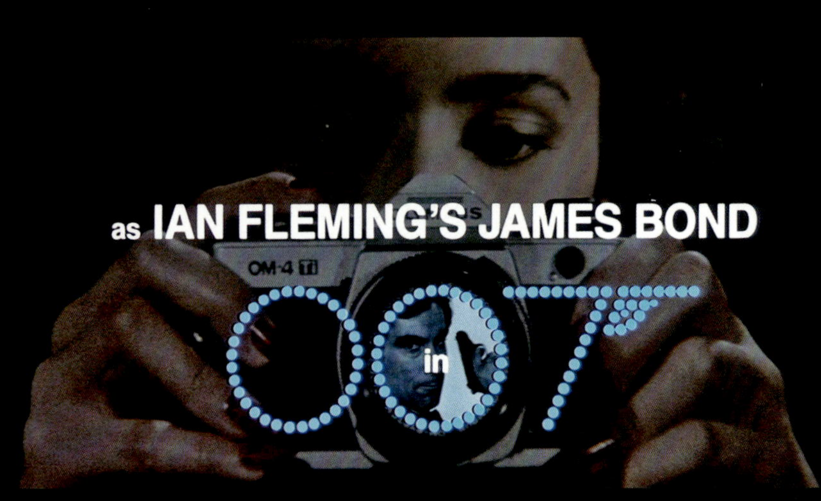

2

"We modeled Bond on the hero of Kurosawa's film Yojimbo, where the samurai comes to town and, without overtly attacking the villain, sows the seeds of distrust, then watches as the villain brings himself down."

—Michael G. Wilson

1. The title sequence was shot by Maurice Binder.

2. The *Licence to Kill* theatrical poster designed by Steven Chorney.

3. Bond finds his friend's new wife, Della Leiter (Priscilla Barnes), murdered. This leads him on a personal mission of revenge. This was Dalton's first scene filmed at the Churubusco Studios in Mexico.

4. Bond discovers Felix Leiter (David Hedison) with a warning note pinned to him: "He disagreed with something that ate him."

5. Director John Glen and script supervisor June Randall watch Pam Bouvier (Carey Lowell) and Bond at Mexico City's Teatro de la Ciudad, which doubles for the Isthmus City Casino.

4

"The area of evil had to be contemporary. We had to ask, What is the great Satan? The answer was the drug lord."

—Richard Maibaum, Screenwriter

5

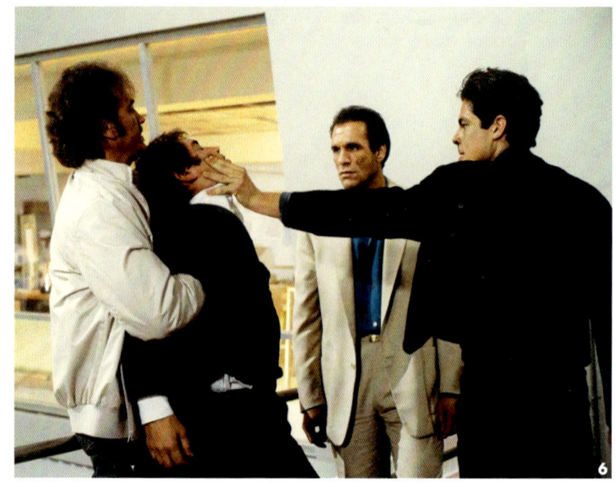

6. At the Olimpatec Meditation Institute that conceals Sanchez's cocaine factory. Sanchez (Robert Davi, second right) realizes that Bond is not to be trusted and orders Dario (Benicio del Toro, right) and Braun (Guy de Saint Cyr) to kill him.

7. As the Olimpatec Meditation Institute explodes, all personnel flee the building.

8. Bond jumps from a plane onto a tanker in pursuit of Sanchez. Simon Crane stunt-doubled for Bond, and Corkey Fornof was the flying double for Pam.

9. Bond destroys the tankers full of liquid cocaine one by one, allowing Chris Corbould to make bigger and bigger explosions.

10. Bond gains revenge for the death of Della Leiter, and the injuries to Felix, by setting Sanchez alight with the present the Leiters gave Bond on their wedding day.

8

9

GoldenEye

1995

RELEASE DATE November 13, 1995 (US) | **RUNNING TIME** 130 minutes

Synopsis

It's 1986: James Bond and Agent 006, Alec Trevelyan, infiltrate a Russian weapons factory, but Trevelyan is killed by Colonel Ourumov while Bond escapes.

Nine years later: General Ourumov and Russian mafia assassin Xenia Onatopp attack the Severnaya satellite control center and gain control of the GoldenEye weapons system in outer space. Only computer programmer Natalya Simonova escapes Severnaya alive.

In St. Petersburg, Bond discovers that Trevelyan had faked his own death, and is planning to use the GoldenEye system to punish Britain for betraying his Cossack parents, who later committed suicide.

After a dramatic tank chase on the streets of St. Petersburg, Bond and Natalya join forces to track Trevelyan to Cuba, and infiltrate his facility. Natalya reprograms GoldenEye, and Bond fights Trevelyan to the death on the installation's giant radio dish.

Cast

JAMES BOND PIERCE BROSNAN
ALEC TREVELYAN SEAN BEAN
NATALYA SIMONOVA IZABELLA SCORUPCO
XENIA ONATOPP FAMKE JANSSEN
JACK WADE JOE DON BAKER
VALENTIN DMITROVICH ZUKOVSKY ROBBIE COLTRANE
BORIS GRISHENKO ALAN CUMMING
M JUDI DENCH

Crew

DIRECTOR MARTIN CAMPBELL
SCREENPLAY JEFFREY CAINE, BRUCE FEIRSTEIN
PRODUCERS MICHAEL G. WILSON, BARBARA BROCCOLI
DIRECTOR OF PHOTOGRAPHY PHIL MÉHEUX
TITLE SONG LYRICS BONO AND THE EDGE
TITLE SONG SUNG BY TINA TURNER

THERE IS NO SUBSTITUTE
007™
ALBERT R. BROCCOLI PRESENTS PIERCE BROSNAN AS JAMES BOND 007 IN "GOLDENEYE" SEAN BEAN IZABELLA SCORUPCO FAMKE JANSSEN AND JOE DON BAKER ASSOCIATE PRODUCER ANTHONY WAYE EDITOR TERRY RAWLINGS
DIRECTOR OF PHOTOGRAPHY PHIL MEHEUX PRODUCTION DESIGNER PETER LAMONT EXECUTIVE PRODUCER TOM PEVSNER WRITTEN BY MICHAEL FRANCE AND JEFFREY CAINE PRODUCED BY MICHAEL G. WILSON AND BARBARA BROCCOLI DIRECTED BY MARTIN CAMPBELL
UNITED ARTISTS
CHRISTMAS '95

1. The titles were designed by Daniel Kleinman.

2. The teaser poster for *GoldenEye*.

3. The pre-title skydiving sequence was designed by B.J. Worth at Big Sky Productions in Montana. It was Worth's suggestion to incorporate the motorcycle into the scene.

4. Martin Asbury's storyboard, which he prepared in consultation with the director, shows how the sequence will develop: Bond jumping off the cliff on his motorbike then free-falling in pursuit of the runaway plane.

"Skydiving next to a diving airplane is quite an amazing experience."

— B.J. Worth, Stuntman

3

PRE-TITLE

68

1st UNIT

TRACKING IN FRONT OF BOND on bike? R.-to L. to CAMERA

162A

SWISS LOCATION A

163

SWISS LOCATION A

ANGLE PLANE drives over CLIFF B on bike following

PAN DOWN as PLANE and BIKE fall!

164

GOLDENEYE

This Storyboard must be returned to the Production Office at the end of your involvement with the film. It is made available to you only and must not be divulged to any third parties. Should it become mislaid, the loss must be reported to the Production Office immediately. This Storyboard and all rights therein are owned exclusively by DANJAQ INC.

© DANJAQ INC. MCMXCIV DATE:........................

4

5. James Bond (Pierce Brosnan) lets rip with a Kalashnikov.

6. Famke Janssen sits behind the wheel of her Ferrari with a camera mounted on the front. A similar courtship-by-driving duel was later seen in *Mission: Impossible 2*.

7. Jeff Kleeman at United Artists suggested the filmmakers should use the fight between the woman and the bodyguard in Jean-Luc Godard's film *Prénom Carmen* (1983) as a reference point for the steam-bath fight between Bond and Xenia Onatopp (Famke Janssen).

5

"Whenever you're dealing with a classic car like the Aston Martin, there's always a production problem, like: are they all going to run? Because you're dealing with a car that's 30 years old."

—Michael G. Wilson

8. James Bond prepares to do battle with a tank on the streets of St. Petersburg.

9. Bond's tank crashes through a wall on the Leavesden back lot. The production bought three Russian tanks at a cost of £9,000 to £14,000 each. There were two Soviet T-54s and one T-55.

10. Puerto Rico may have the world's largest spherical radar-radio telescope, but it wasn't submerged under a giant lake. Derek Meddings's team built a miniature of the dish, but because the real structure was so enormous their 1/20 scale model measured 50 feet across.

8

9

A•S
A•S

Tomorrow Never Dies

1997

RELEASE DATE December 9, 1997 (UK) | **RUNNING TIME** 119 minutes

Synopsis

While James Bond spies on a terrorist arms bazaar, he identifies "techno-terrorist" Henry Gupta, who is buying a stolen American GPS encoder. As Bond hijacks a Russian plane carrying nuclear torpedoes, Gupta escapes with the encoder during the confusion.

Gupta is working for media baron Elliot Carver, who plans to provoke war between China and the United Kingdom. Gupta uses the encoder to send the British frigate HMS *Devonshire* off-course into Chinese waters, where Carver's stealth ship, commanded by Stamper, sinks the frigate with a sea drill and steals one of its missiles. Bond has 48 hours to investigate the sinking before the British and Chinese go to war. Bond investigates Carver in Hamburg; seduces Carver's wife, Paris; and steals the GPS encoder. Carver orders assassin Dr. Kaufman to kill Paris and Bond. Paris dies, but Bond kills Kaufman and escapes.

Bond travels to the South China Sea and discovers that one of the missiles is missing from the wreck of the HMS *Devonshire*. Wai Lin, a Chinese agent on the same case, and Bond are captured by Stamper and taken to Carver's headquarters in Ho Chi Minh City, but they escape and team up. They board Carver's stealth ship to prevent him firing the stolen British missile at Beijing. In the final confrontation, Bond detonates an explosive, exposing the ship on radar to the Royal Navy, and kills Carver with the sea drill.

Cast

JAMES BOND PIERCE BROSNAN
ELLIOT CARVER JONATHAN PRYCE
WAI LIN MICHELLE YEOH
PARIS CARVER TERI HATCHER
JACK WADE JOE DON BAKER
STAMPER GÖTZ OTTO
GUPTA RICKY JAY

Crew

DIRECTOR ROGER SPOTTISWOODE
SCREENPLAY BRUCE FEIRSTEIN
PRODUCERS MICHAEL G. WILSON, BARBARA BROCCOLI
DIRECTOR OF PHOTOGRAPHY ROBERT ELSWIT
MUSIC DAVID ARNOLD
TITLE SONG SUNG BY SHERYL CROW

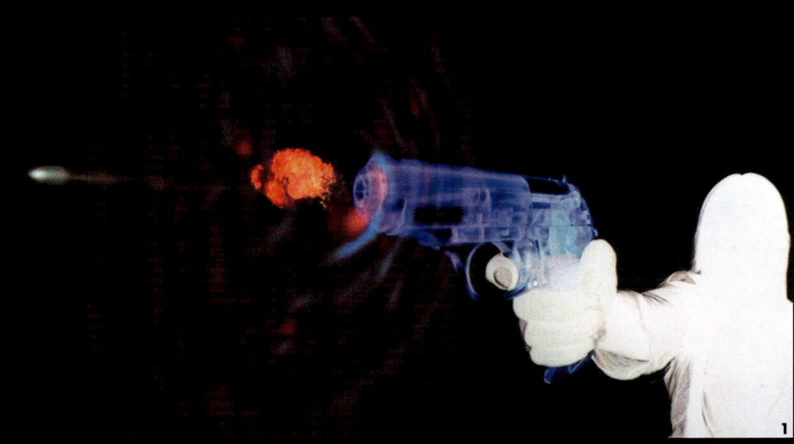

1

"Wai Lin is not the feminine equivalent of James Bond; she's the flip side of James Bond. She has a very different style and a very different attitude. They make a good pair."

—Michael G. Wilson

VARIATIONS FOR HELICOPTER JUMP

3

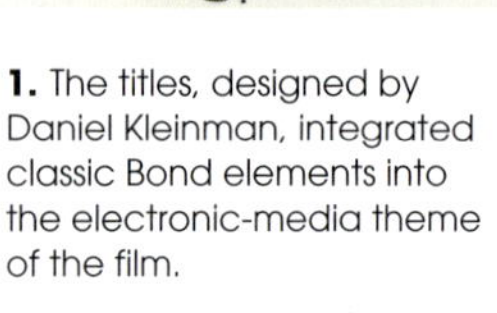

1. The titles, designed by Daniel Kleinman, integrated classic Bond elements into the electronic-media theme of the film.

2. The international poster art for *Tomorrow Never Dies*.

3. Martin Asbury's storyboard shows various camera angles that could be used for the jump.

"The action is such a huge part of the movie and it's very important it's done properly. Directors really have to trust the second-unit director, otherwise part of their movie just isn't going to work."

—Vic Armstrong, Second Unit Director

4. Stuntman Jean-Pierre Goy jumps over a helicopter on a BMW R1200C Cruiser, with a dummy Wai Lin attached to his back. The swirling blades of the helicopter were added in post-production using CGI.

5. Bond and Wai Lin (Michelle Yeoh) slide the BMW R1200C underneath the blades of the helicopter.

6. After a series of death-defying adventures, Bond and Wai Lin cool off in a street shower as their icy relationship thaws.

7. The bicycle-shop fight sequence allowed Michelle Yeoh, a major star of Asian action cinema, to show off her considerable martial-arts talents, also signaling that her character was in no way going to be subservient to James Bond.

8. Filming the model version of Carver's stealth boat in the giant water tank at Baja Studios in Mexico, alongside mock-ups of Phuket's distinctive islands. Miniature effects supervisor John Richardson: "The stealth boat model was 30 feet long, and weighed about three and a half tons."

9. Bond and Wai Lin prepare for their climactic incursion into Carver's fearsome stealth boat, with Bond coming to grips with his new firearm, the 16-round Walther P99.

"Bond lives in a world set 30 seconds into the future."

—Bruce Feirstein, Screenwriter

The World Is Not Enough

1999

RELEASE DATE November 8, 1999 (US) | **RUNNING TIME** 128 minutes

Synopsis

Following the murder of her father, oil magnate Sir Robert King, Elektra is assigned a bodyguard—MI6's top agent, James Bond. Sir Robert, an old friend of M's, has been assassinated by terrorist Renard, who also seems to be targeting the 800-mile King pipeline, under construction from Azerbaijan to bring oil to the West. Freelance terrorist Renard has a bullet lodged in his skull following a run-in with 009: slowly dying, he feels no pain. Bond and Elektra become emotionally involved, but it transpires that Elektra, previously the victim of a kidnapping plot by Renard, seduced him and has engineered the takeover of her father's business empire. Elektra kidnaps M and plans to detonate a nuclear explosion in Istanbul, contaminating the Bosphorus and ensuring the King pipeline is the sole oil route west. Bond, aided by atomic physicist Dr. Christmas Jones, kills Elektra and Renard, rescues M, and prevents the cataclysm.

Cast

JAMES BOND PIERCE BROSNAN
ELEKTRA SOPHIE MARCEAU
RENARD ROBERT CARLYLE
CHRISTMAS JONES DENISE RICHARDS
VALENTIN ZUKOVSKY ROBBIE COLTRANE
M JUDI DENCH
Q DESMOND LLEWELYN

Crew

DIRECTOR MICHAEL APTED
SCREENPLAY NEAL PURVIS & ROBERT WADE, BRUCE FEIRSTEIN
PRODUCERS MICHAEL G. WILSON, BARBARA BROCCOLI
DIRECTOR OF PHOTOGRAPHY ADRIAN BIDDLE
TITLE SONG SUNG BY GARBAGE

1

ALBERT R. BROCCOLI'S EON PRODUCTIONS PRESENTS
PIERCE BROSNAN AS IAN FLEMING'S JAMES BOND 007
The World Is Not Enough
007
ALBERT R. BROCCOLI'S EON PRODUCTIONS PRESENTS PIERCE BROSNAN AS IAN FLEMING'S JAMES BOND 007 IN "THE WORLD IS NOT ENOUGH" SOPHIE MARCEAU ROBERT CARLYLE
DENISE RICHARDS ROBBIE COLTRANE AND JUDI DENCH COSTUME DESIGNER LINDY HEMMING MUSIC BY DAVID ARNOLD EDITOR JIM CLARK DIRECTOR OF PHOTOGRAPHY ADRIAN BIDDLE BSC PRODUCTION DESIGNER PETER LAMONT LINE PRODUCER ANTHONY WAYE
STORY BY NEAL PURVIS & ROBERT WADE SCREENPLAY BY NEAL PURVIS & ROBERT WADE AND BRUCE FEIRSTEIN PRODUCED BY MICHAEL G. WILSON AND BARBARA BROCCOLI DIRECTED BY MICHAEL APTED
TITLE SONG PERFORMED BY GARBAGE
DISTRIBUTED BY MGM DISTRIBUTION CO.

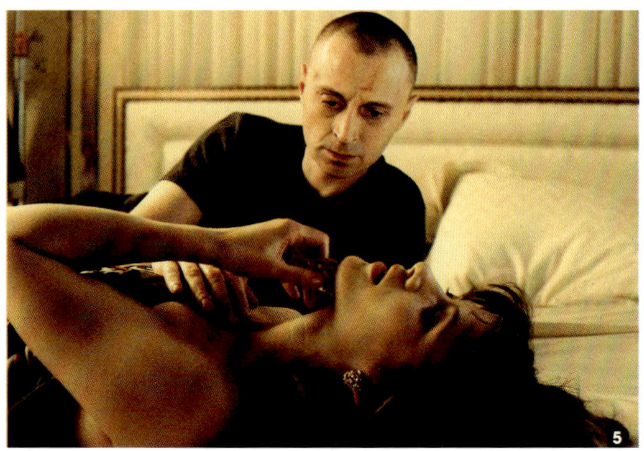

1. The oily, psychedelic imagery of the title sequence, inspired by Maurice Binder's iconic titles, was designed by Daniel Kleinman.

2. US final poster artwork for *The World Is Not Enough*, designed by Diane Reynolds.

3. The buzz-saw helicopter wreaks havoc on Zukovsky's Caviar Fishery, narrowly missing Bond. The fishery was created in the paddock tank at Pinewood, which was enlarged 50 percent to accommodate the huge set.

"Audiences now are very demanding. They pay for their seat and they want to have a spectacle, a show, but also a human story."

—Sophie Marceau

4. Pierce Brosnan and Sophie Marceau fool around during rehearsals on the villa bedroom set on C Stage at Pinewood.

5. Elektra King (Sophie Marceau) tries to instill some feeling into terrorist Renard (Robert Carlyle), who has lost his sense of touch. Director Michael Apted: "I'd had the idea of using ice and Sophie developed the thing of kissing him with the ice. She's really good to work with because she's uninhibited."

6. M (Judi Dench) slaps her friend, now her betrayer, in the pipeline control center, Turkey, on C Stage.

7. As the capstan turns on the torture chair, a rod slides out to slowly break Bond's neck. Bond: "The World Is Not Enough." Elektra: "Foolish sentiment." Bond: "Family motto."

Die Another Day

2002

RELEASE DATE November 18, 2002 (UK) | **RUNNING TIME** 133 minutes

Synopsis

In North Korea, Bond kills Colonel Moon, who is trading weapons for African blood diamonds, and disfigures Moon's henchman Zao in the process. Bond is captured and spends 14 months in prison before being exchanged for Zao, who had been captured by the British. MI6 believe Bond has cracked under torture, so he is disavowed.

Bond tracks Zao to a Havana clinic, where he meets NSA agent Jinx Johnson, and finds out Zao is receiving DNA therapy to alter his appearance. After Zao escapes from the clinic, Bond follows the diamonds to London, and then to billionaire Gustav Graves. M also suspects Graves—she planted agent Miranda Frost as Graves's assistant—and gives Bond back his 00 status.

In Iceland Graves unveils Icarus, a powerful laser satellite. Working together, Bond and Jinx discover that Graves is actually Moon; the colonel didn't die in Korea and altered his appearance with gene therapy. Moon plans to use Icarus to help North Korea invade the South, but Bond and Jinx stow away on his cargo plane, where Jinx kills Frost, who had switched her allegiance to Moon, and Bond kills Moon, so preventing the invasion.

Cast

JAMES BOND PIERCE BROSNAN
JINX JOHNSON HALLE BERRY
GUSTAV GRAVES TOBY STEPHENS
MIRANDA FROST ROSAMUND PIKE
ZAO RICK YUNE
DAMIAN FALCO MICHAEL MADSEN
COLONEL MOON WILL YUN LEE

Crew

DIRECTOR LEE TAMAHORI
SCREENPLAY NEAL PURVIS & ROBERT WADE
PRODUCERS MICHAEL G. WILSON, BARBARA BROCCOLI
DIRECTOR OF PHOTOGRAPHY DAVID TATTERSALL
TITLE SONG SUNG BY MADONNA

PIERCE BROSNAN
007
DIE ANOTHER DAY
www.jamesbond.com

1. Daniel Kleinman's title sequence marks a break with tradition by showing 007's torture during his incarceration in North Korea. It was the first time that a Bond title sequence had been used to advance the movie's story.

2. *Die Another Day*'s teaser poster.

3. Bond entices Jinx with a cocktail as Brosnan and Halle Berry convince the audience they're sweltering in Cuba rather than freezing in Cádiz.

"Pierce is the knight in shining armor—which is the tuxedo and the dangerous smile."

—Rick Yune

4. Bond and Gustav Graves (Toby Stephens) fight through the corridors of the Blades Club after their fencing match turns into an action-packed sword fight. The sequence was choreographed by former Olympic fencer Bob Anderson, who staged classic sword battles for the *Star Wars* films and the *Lord of the Rings* trilogy, and had been a stuntman on *From Russia with Love*.

5. Not shaken, not stirred: Bond cleans his Walther P99 and sips whiskey as director Lee Tamahori lines up a shot.

6. Brosnan gets ready for a close-up while filming on the counterfeit ice lake at Burford. The car chase sequence turns into a duel on ice.

7

"Jinx is very feisty and she's tough. She is Bond's equal."

—Halle Berry

7. Halle Berry is tied up to a modern laser table, in a homage to *Goldfinger*.

8. Jinx and Miranda Frost (Rosamund Pike) do battle in the Antonov cargo plane's hold. Training to play a Gold medal-winning Olympic fencer was interesting for Pike: "It is a fantastic sport for an actor. Many of the drama schools train people in it because it's terrific for movement."

9. Graves has Bond in a throat hold during the climactic fight. Graves's high-tech suit began life as a large glove, before being upgraded. Tamahori: "I said, 'A big glove isn't that exciting,' and they said, 'Why don't we add a hundred thousand volts, give it defensive capabilities, Taser-light killing abilities, track-ball control—so he could wear it as a fighting combat unit as well?'"

8

"Bond movies are always measured by the strength of the villains in them."

—Lee Tamahori, Director

9

Casino Royale

2006

RELEASE DATE November 14, 2006 (UK) | **RUNNING TIME** 144 minutes

Synopsis

After becoming a 00 agent, James Bond hunts down a bomb maker in Madagascar, which leads him to shady financier Alex Dimitrios in the Bahamas, and then to a plot to blow up the prototype Skyfleet airliner at Miami airport. By preventing the bombing, Bond leaves criminal banker Le Chiffre on the verge of bankruptcy—Le Chiffre lost his clients' money by betting on Skyfleet's failure on the stock market.

Le Chiffre sets up a high-stakes poker game in Montenegro to win back the lost money. Bond attends with Treasury agent Vesper Lynd and wins, but Le Chiffre kidnaps Lynd and tortures Bond in an attempt to regain the winnings. They are saved when Mr. White, a senior figure in terrorist organization Quantum, kills Le Chiffre. However, Lynd is secretly working for White and has made a deal with him to save Bond's life.

In love with Lynd, Bond resigns from MI6 and travels to Venice with her. There, he realizes she has betrayed him and stolen the money. After a gunfight with Quantum's men in a collapsing Venetian villa, Lynd lets herself drown because she cannot bear the burden of her guilt. Bond pursues White and shoots him in the leg, then introduces himself: "The name's Bond, James Bond."

Cast

JAMES BOND DANIEL CRAIG
VESPER LYND EVA GREEN
LE CHIFFRE MADS MIKKELSEN
M JUDI DENCH
FELIX LEITER JEFFREY WRIGHT
MATHIS GIANCARLO GIANNINI
SOLANGE CATERINA MURINO

Crew

DIRECTOR MARTIN CAMPBELL
SCREENPLAY NEAL PURVIS & ROBERT WADE, PAUL HAGGIS
PRODUCERS MICHAEL G. WILSON, BARBARA BROCCOLI
DIRECTOR OF PHOTOGRAPHY PHIL MÉHEUX
TITLE SONG SUNG BY CHRIS CORNELL

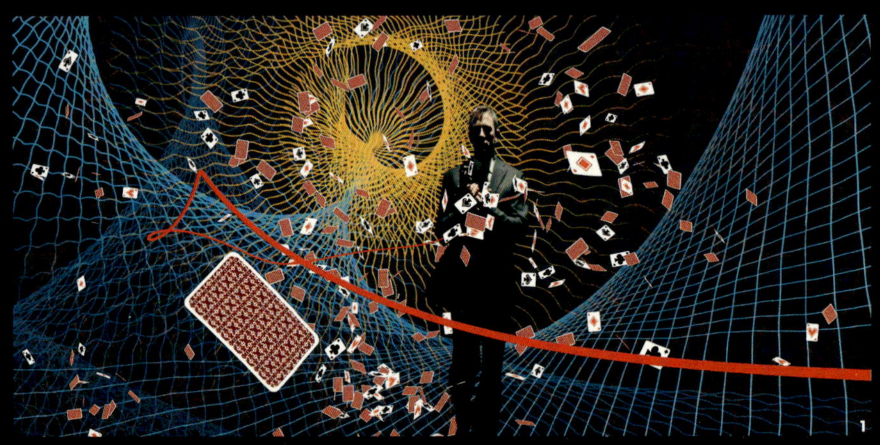

CASINO ROYALE

007

24. NOVEMBER

CasinoRoyaleMovie.com

COLUMBIA PICTURES

1. Daniel Kleinman's title sequence forgoes the alluring women of previous films, and uses the designs and iconography of the playing cards that will be an integral part of the film.

2. The *Casino Royale* teaser poster designed by Vox and Associates, photographed by Greg Williams, captures the glamour of the poker table and the deadly allure of Bond. The release poster featured Bond in a tuxedo and undone bow tie, a more rough-and-ready image in keeping with this new Bond's less polished attitude.

3. Bond (Daniel Craig) makes a death-defying leap: if you look carefully you can see the safety wire running up to the crane above.

"When you see Vesper for the first time you can't really read her. She's an enigma."

—Eva Green

4. In his tuxedo, Daniel Craig looks every inch the suave, sophisticated spy that Ian Fleming envisioned.

5. Bond producer Michael G. Wilson tutors Daniel Craig on the intricacies of how to play Texas Hold 'em.

6. Bond comforts Vesper Lynd (Eva Green) after she witnesses him kill a man with his bare hands.

7. Director Martin Campbell briefs the poker players in a break between takes. With ten players around the table, this sequence became one of the most difficult for the director to shoot.

8

9

10

"I had a stunt double. I did the bits that hurt. He did the bits that fucking hurt. But that's the thing with this Bond. He bleeds, goes down, and gets up again."

—Daniel Craig

8. Le Chiffre (Mads Mikkelsen) tortures Bond with a knotted rope. The scene made it past the censors because the eye-wincing action is kept offscreen.

9. Vesper Lynd locks herself in the elevator cage of the crumbling Venetian villa, and moments later she's plunged into the water. Vesper cannot live with her betrayal of Bond, who has fallen in love with her. Underwater, Vesper kisses Bond's hand to comfort him, just as he had kissed her hand in the shower to comfort her.

10. In the film's coda, set on Lake Como in Italy, Bond shoots Mr. White (Jesper Christensen) and announces his presence.

Quantum of Solace

2008

RELEASE DATE October 29, 2008 (UK) | **RUNNING TIME** 106 minutes

Synopsis

Quantum of Solace starts 10 minutes after the end of *Casino Royale.* Bond's search for answers behind Vesper's betrayal leads him to uncover QUANTUM, a sinister organization whose tentacles spread across the globe, with double agents buried within the British government, MI6, and the CIA. Evidence takes him to Haiti, where he meets Camille. She is an agent who has her own vengeance-fuelled agenda, to avenge her family's deaths at the hands of former Bolivian dictator General Medrano. Posing as the girlfriend of faux-environmentalist Dominic Greene, she becomes suspicious of his land acquisition and business relationship with Medrano. With Bond by her side, they discover Greene is part of QUANTUM, an organization that is secretly appropriating all of Bolivia's water supply and replacing its left-of-center president with a more pliable leader.

Cast

JAMES BOND DANIEL CRAIG
CAMILLE MONTES OLGA KURYLENKO
DOMINIC GREENE MATHIEU AMALRIC
M JUDI DENCH
RENÉ MATHIS GIANCARLO GIANNINI
AGENT FIELDS GEMMA ARTERTON
FELIX LEITER JEFFREY WRIGHT

Crew

DIRECTOR MARC FORSTER
SCREENPLAY PAUL HAGGIS, NEAL PURVIS & ROBERT WADE
PRODUCERS MICHAEL G. WILSON, BARBARA BROCCOLI
DIRECTOR OF PHOTOGRAPHY ROBERTO SCHAEFER
PRODUCTION DESIGNER DENNIS GASSNER
TITLE SONG SUNG BY JACK WHITE & ALICIA KEYS

QUANTUM
OF
SOLACE
007
OCTOBER 31
007.COM
COLUMBIA PICTURES

1. Title sequence, codirected by Ben Radatz and Tim Fisher from design collective MK12.

2. Poster for *Quantum of Solace*, photography by Greg Williams.

3. Bobby Holland Hanton, stunt double for Bond, leaping across the rooftops of Siena in pursuit of QUANTUM mole Mitchell (Glenn Foster), and being followed by stunt cameraman Diz Sharpe.

4. Camille (Olga Kurylenko) looks on as James Bond dumps the body of René Mathis (Giancarlo Giannini). "He wouldn't care," says Bond.

5. M (Judi Dench) and Bond are horrified by Fields's (Gemma Arterton) death.

6. Bond and Greene (Mathieu Amalric) fighting as the hotel burns around them, filmed at Pinewood Studios.

7. Having finally killed Medrano, Camille's childhood fear of fire traps her in the room. Bond helps her escape.

"I don't think there's enough money in the British government to ever turn MI6 into one like ours. I think they'd be terribly jealous."

—Judi Dench

7

Skyfall

2012

RELEASE DATE October 23, 2012 (UK) | **RUNNING TIME** 143 minutes

Synopsis

James Bond chases assassin Patrice through the streets of Istanbul to recover a flash drive containing the names of every MI6 and NATO agent embedded in terrorist organizations around the world. As Bond and Patrice fight on top of a moving train, on M's orders field agent Eve attempts to shoot Patrice, but she hits Bond. He falls 300 feet into the water below and is presumed dead. MI6 is attacked, forcing M to relocate the agency underground. These events cause her authority and position to be challenged by Mallory, the new chairman of the Intelligence and Security Committee.

Bond returns, broken and full of doubts. He fails MI6's physical and psychological tests, but M lies to him and tells him he has passed, and she sends him on a mission to track down Patrice in Shanghai. Assuming Patrice's identity, Bond follows clues that lead him to femme fatale Severine in Macau, and then to her master, Silva, on an abandoned island. Silva is a former MI6 agent seeking revenge for M's betrayal of him, but Bond captures him before he can carry out his plan. As M goes in front of a board of inquiry, and Q tries to hack into Silva's computer, Silva escapes and Bond goes in pursuit. Silva attacks the board of inquiry, but Bond gets M out safely and drives her north to his ancestral home in Scotland, Skyfall. With the help of gamekeeper Kincade, Bond and M defend Skyfall from Silva's assault, and defeat him, but not before M receives a fatal wound.

Later, Bond reports to Mallory—the new M—and is ready to take on his next mission.

Cast

JAMES BOND DANIEL CRAIG
RAOUL SILVA JAVIER BARDEM
M JUDI DENCH
GARETH MALLORY RALPH FIENNES
EVE MONEYPENNY NAOMIE HARRIS
Q BEN WHISHAW

Crew

DIRECTOR SAM MENDES
SCREENPLAY NEAL PURVIS & ROBERT WADE, JOHN LOGAN
PRODUCERS MICHAEL G. WILSON, BARBARA BROCCOLI
DIRECTOR OF PHOTOGRAPHY ROGER DEAKINS
MUSIC THOMAS NEWMAN
TITLE SONG SUNG BY ADELE

SKYFALL
007
OCTOBER 26
MGM
/skyfallmovie
COLUMBIA PICTURES

1. James Bond ready for action in the opening scene set in Istanbul.

2. The teaser poster for *Skyfall*.

3. The second unit, directed by Alexander Witt, spent one month rehearsing and setting up the action and stunt work in Turkey, and then filmed for two months.

4. Bond enters the floating casino—stunning production design by Dennis Gassner.

"Silva is a man full of pain, full of suffering, full of frustration, who wants to fix his situation by doing very violent acts. I could perfectly understand who he was and that helped me to portray him."

—Javier Bardem

5. The first meeting of Q (Ben Whishaw) and Bond is in front of J.M.W. Turner's *The Fighting Temeraire* at the National Gallery. Q comments on the painting, but it could also apply to Bond: "The grand old warship being ignominiously hauled away for scrap… The inevitability of time, don't you think?"

6. Silva (Javier Bardem) in the computer room of the dead city.

7. Bond has rescued M (Judi Dench), but he is also using her as bait for Silva.

8. Sam Mendes directs M's death, with Daniel Craig and Judi Dench.

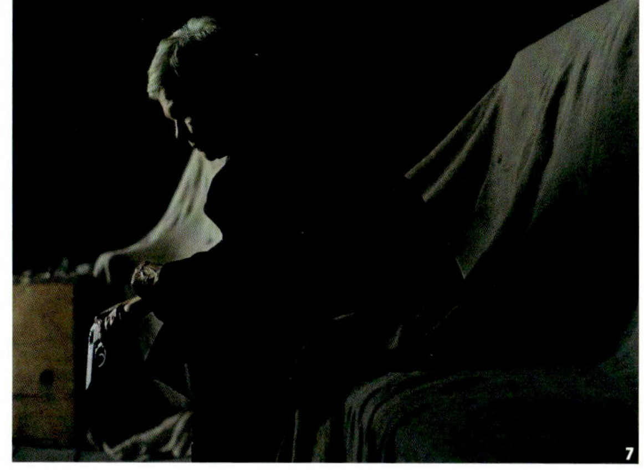

Spectre

2015

RELEASE DATE October 26, 2015 (UK) | **RUNNING TIME** 148 minutes

Synopsis

On a rogue mission in Mexico City Bond kills an assassin. Back in London, Bond is grounded by M but confides in Moneypenny that he was acting on orders from the previous M before she died.

Bond travels to Rome and seduces the assassin's widow to infiltrate a secret meeting, but their leader, Franz Oberhauser, reveals Bond's presence. The terrifying Mr. Hinx pursues Bond in a car chase.

In Austria, Bond meets his old nemesis Mr. White and makes a promise to keep White's daughter safe in exchange for leading him to Oberhauser. The daughter, Dr. Madeleine Swann, is reluctant to help, but after Bond rescues her from Hinx she agrees. She reveals the secret organization is SPECTRE.

Swann leads Bond to Tangier, and from there they journey by train to a desert location. Swann makes Bond question the life he has chosen for himself. Hinx appears and a vicious fight ensues. At a high-tech facility in the desert Bond and Swann meet Oberhauser. He amasses information to manipulate events and is about to gain control of a global surveillance network. After Oberhauser tortures Bond and reveals himself to be Ernst Stavro Blofeld, Bond and Swann escape and destroy the base.

In London Bond debriefs M, is captured by Blofeld, then rescues Swann. Bond has the opportunity to kill Blofeld but decides to let him live. Bond joins Swann, leaving his old life behind.

Cast

JAMES BOND DANIEL CRAIG
FRANZ OBERHAUSER / BLOFELD CHRISTOPH WALTZ
DR. MADELEINE SWANN LÉA SEYDOUX
M RALPH FIENNES
LUCIA SCIARRA MONICA BELLUCCI

Crew

DIRECTOR SAM MENDES
SCREENPLAY JOHN LOGAN, NEAL PURVIS & ROBERT WADE, JEZ BUTTERWORTH
PRODUCERS MICHAEL G. WILSON, BARBARA BROCCOLI
DIRECTOR OF PHOTOGRAPHY HOYTE VAN HOYTEMA
TITLE SONG SUNG BY SAM SMITH

ALBERT R. BROCCOLI'S EON PRODUCTIONS PRESENTS DANIEL CRAIG AS IAN FLEMING'S JAMES BOND 007 IN
SPECTRE
007
ALBERT R. BROCCOLI'S EON PRODUCTIONS PRESENTS DANIEL CRAIG AS IAN FLEMING'S JAMES BOND 007 IN "SPECTRE" CHRISTOPH WALTZ LÉA SEYDOUX BEN WHISHAW NAOMIE HARRIS
DAVE BAUTISTA WITH MONICA BELLUCCI AND RALPH FIENNES
MGM
#SPECTRE
007.COM
FEATURING "WRITING'S ON THE WALL" PERFORMED BY SAM SMITH
OCTOBER 26
EXPERIENCE IT IN IMAX

3

"We design something like 200 sets, but only shoot 100. You're seeing the best of each option. We're not here to stand on the wrong sets. We're here to stand on the right sets." —Chris Lowe, Supervising Art Director

4

1. The title sequence was designed by Daniel Kleinman.

2. The poster for *Spectre*.

3. Concept art by Greg Fangeaux for the Day of the Dead parade. From October 2014, 60 people spent six months making the dresses, as well as designing and painting 450 masks.

4. Bond cannot escape Hinx (Dave Bautista). Gary Powell: "We tested and rehearsed a 150-foot jump with both cars, in preparation for jumping over two ancient statues in Rome, but the authorities refused permission—they just spent millions of euros restoring the statues—so we cut the jump."

5. Bond, in the plane, plays "chicken" with Hinx and his convoy. For this shot, the plane is hung from wires between two cranes to control the descent. A similar wire rig was used on *Thunderball* (1965) to smoothly land the Vulcan in the water.

6

7

6. On a train in the middle of the Moroccan desert, Bond finds out that he does not have to teach Swann (Léa Seydoux), the daughter of an assassin, how to use a gun.

7. Hinx and Bond battle to the death.

8. Oberhauser, a figure from Bond's past who now goes by the name Ernst Stavro Blofeld (Christoph Waltz), prepares to torture Bond. Bond tells him, "Get on with it, then. Nothing can be as painful as listening to you talk."

"In* Casino Royale *Bond fell in love, got double-crossed, and decided that he could never have an emotional life again. In* Spectre*, he meets Madeleine Swann, who asks him, 'Is this really what you want? Living in the shadows. Hunting. Being hunted. Always looking behind you. Always alone.' For the first time since Vesper Lynd, he sees the possibility of another life."

—Barbara Broccoli, Producer

No Time to Die

2021

RELEASE DATE September 30, 2021 (UK) | **RUNNING TIME** 163 minutes

Synopsis
Bond has left active service and is enjoying a tranquil life in Jamaica. His peace is short-lived when his old friend Felix Leiter from the CIA turns up asking for help. The mission to rescue a kidnapped scientist turns out to be far more treacherous than expected, leading Bond onto the trail of a mysterious villain armed with dangerous new technology.

The Title
Barbara Broccoli: "We were struggling to find a title. We wanted a title that wouldn't give away anything but would be understandable, and after you see the movie, have a deeper resonance, because that's often what Fleming titles are all about. I came up with this brainwave—thinking I was terribly clever. Of course, when we did the title search, I realized I hadn't made it up, but had already seen it. *No Time to Die* was the UK title of one of Cubby's films, *Tank Force* (1958). The connection to Cubby made me love the title even more. So I'm not clever, it's him."

Cast
JAMES BOND DANIEL CRAIG
LYUTSIFER SAFIN RAMI MALEK
MADELEINE SWANN LÉA SEYDOUX
NOMI LASHANA LYNCH
M RALPH FIENNES
BLOFELD CHRISTOPH WALTZ
Q BEN WHISHAW

Crew
DIRECTOR CARY JOJI FUKUNAGA
SCREENPLAY NEAL PURVIS & ROBERT WADE, CARY JOJI FUKUNAGA, PHOEBE WALLER-BRIDGE
PRODUCERS MICHAEL G. WILSON, BARBARA BROCCOLI
PRODUCTION DESIGNER MARK TILDESLEY
DIRECTOR OF PHOTOGRAPHY LINUS SANDGREN
MUSIC HANS ZIMMER, STEVE MAZZARO
TITLE SONG SUNG BY BILLIE EILISH & FINNEAS O'CONNELL

1

NO
TIME
TO
DIE

007

NOVEMBER

1. The title sequence was designed by Daniel Kleinman.

2. The teaser poster for *No Time to Die*.

3. Madeleine (Coline Defaud) drags Safin (Rami Malek) across the snow, thinking he is dead, but then he recovers. The movie was shot on 35mm film with some sequences shot on a 65mm IMAX, as seen here.

4. SPECTRE surrounds Bond and Madeleine (Léa Seydoux) in the Piazza San Giovanna Batista, but the Aston Martin DB5 has some tricks up its sleeve. It fires bullets from its front light housings and spews a smokescreen as it spins around, then makes its escape.

"In this film we see Bond's faults as well as his strength and power."

—Léa Seydoux

5. Nomi (Lashana Lynch) snatches Valdo Obruchev (David Dencik) from Bond. Valdo has developed Heracles, a poison that targets a person's unique DNA. Set decorator Véronique Melery: "Valdo and Q are diametrically opposed: Q, generous and humble; Valdo, a selfish psychopathological coward."

6. After Bond and Paloma (Ana de Armas) crash the Spectre party, the DNA-targeting poison is released to kill Bond. However, Valdo has double-crossed SPECTRE, and the gas kills the SPECTRE agents. In the ensuing chaos Paloma shows that she is a deadly asset.

7

7. Bond is distraught at the thought that harm may come to Mathilde (Lisa-Dorah Sonnet), so he hides his daughter with Madeleine while he fights Safin's men.

8. With missiles on their way to destroy the heavily fortified base, Bond must go back and open the blast doors to ensure the deadly poison is eradicated.

9. Bond and Safin face off in the poison garden. Safin breaks the vial around his neck ensuring that even if Bond escapes, he could never touch Madeleine or Mathilde again without causing their death.

10. Bond fights his way to the control tower so he can open the blast doors. Oliver Schneider: "It is a one-shot sequence in a stairwell with Daniel doing everything—shooting 15 or more guys, and throwing grenades." After Bond's death, M suggests an epitaph for him from Jack London, which was also used by Mary Goodnight in Fleming's novel *You Only Live Twice*: "I shall not waste my days in trying to prolong them. I shall use my time."

9

"Everybody has lost their family—the villain, the heroine, and the hero—so when Bond and Madeleine become a family it is a great psychologically healing moment for them. Even the villain is trying to have a family. Everybody is after the same thing."

—Michael G. Wilson

10

Imprint

JAMES BOND, 007, and related James Bond copyrights and/or trademarks authorized for use by Metro-Goldwyn-Mayer Studios Inc., exclusive licensee of London Operations LLC. © 2025 Metro-Goldwyn-Mayer Studios Inc. All Rights Reserved.

DR NO © 1962 Metro-Goldwyn-Mayer Studios Inc. and Danjaq, LLC. FROM RUSSIA WITH LOVE © 1963 Metro-Goldwyn-Mayer Studios Inc. and Danjaq, LLC. GOLDFINGER © 1964 Metro-Goldwyn-Mayer Studios Inc. and Danjaq, LLC. THUNDERBALL © 1965 Metro-Goldwyn-Mayer Studios Inc. and Danjaq, LLC. YOU ONLY LIVE TWICE © 1967 Metro-Goldwyn-Mayer Studios Inc. and Danjaq, LLC. ON HER MAJESTY'S SECRET SERVICE © 1969 Metro-Goldwyn-Mayer Studios Inc. and Danjaq, LLC. DIAMONDS ARE FOREVER © 1971 Metro-Goldwyn-Mayer Studios Inc. and Danjaq, LLC. LIVE AND LET DIE © 1973 Metro-Goldwyn-Mayer Studios Inc. and Danjaq, LLC. THE MAN WITH THE GOLDEN GUN © 1974 Metro-Goldwyn-Mayer Studios Inc. and Danjaq, LLC. THE SPY WHO LOVED ME © 1977 Metro-Goldwyn-Mayer Studios Inc. and Danjaq, LLC. MOON-RAKER © 1979 Metro-Goldwyn-Mayer Studios Inc. and Danjaq, LLC. FOR YOUR EYES ONLY © 1981 Metro-Goldwyn-Mayer Studios Inc. and Danjaq, LLC. OCTOPUSSY © 1983 Metro-Goldwyn-Mayer Studios Inc. and Danjaq, LLC. A VIEW TO A KILL © 1985 Metro-Goldwyn-Mayer Studios Inc. and Danjaq, LLC. THE LIVING DAYLIGHTS © 1987 Metro-Goldwyn-Mayer Studios Inc. and Danjaq, LLC. LICENCE TO KILL © 1989 Metro-Goldwyn-Mayer Studios Inc. and Danjaq, LLC. GOLDENEYE © 1995 Seventeen Leasing Corp. and Danjaq, LLC. TOMORROW NEVER DIES © 1997 Eighteen Leasing Corp. and Danjaq, LLC. THE WORLD IS NOT ENOUGH © 1999 United Artists Corporation and Danjaq, LLC. DIE ANOTHER DAY © 2002 United Artists Corporation and Danjaq, LLC. CASINO ROYALE © 2006 United Artists Corporation and Danjaq, LLC. QUANTUM OF SOLACE © 2008 Metro-Goldwyn-Mayer Studios Inc. and Danjaq, LLC. SKYFALL © 2012 Metro-Goldwyn-Mayer Studios Inc., Danjaq, LLC and Columbia Pictures Industries, Inc. SPECTRE © 2015 Metro-Goldwyn-Mayer Studios Inc., Danjaq, LLC and Columbia Pictures Industries, Inc. NO TIME TO DIE © 2021 Danjaq, LLC and Metro-Goldwyn-Mayer Studios Inc. CASINO ROYALE © 1967 Famous Artists Productions Ltd and Danjaq, LLC. NEVER SAY NEVER AGAIN © 1983 NSNA Company. All Rights Reserved.

All images in this book are supplied courtesy of Amazon MGM Studios and the Margaret Herrick Library, except for the following:
Pages 1, 162 top and bottom, 163 bottom, 164 top, 165, 171 top: © Greg Williams
Pages 42, 43 top and bottom, 44/45, 57 bottom, 59 top, 68 bottom, 69 top and bottom: Courtesy British Film Institute, Posters and Designs, London

EACH AND EVERY TASCHEN BOOK PLANTS A SEED!
Each year, we offset our annual carbon emissions with carbon credits at the Instituto Terra, a reforestation program in Minas Gerais, Brazil, founded by Lélia and Sebastião Salgado. To find out more about this ecological partnership, please check: taschen.com/institutoterra.
Inspiration: unlimited.
Carbon footprint: (almost) zero.

Want to see more? Visit taschen.com to view our current publications, browse our latest magazine, and subscribe to our newsletter.

© 2026 TASCHEN GmbH
Hohenzollernring 53, D-50672 Köln
taschen.com

Editor Paul Duncan/Wordsmith Solutions

Printed in Italy
ISBN 978-3-7544-0065-4

PAGE 1
James Bond (Daniel Craig) completes his first kill in *Casino Royale* (2006), which segues into the gun-barrel sequence.

PAGE 2
James Bond (Sean Connery) and his Aston Martin DB5 in *Goldfinger* (1964).

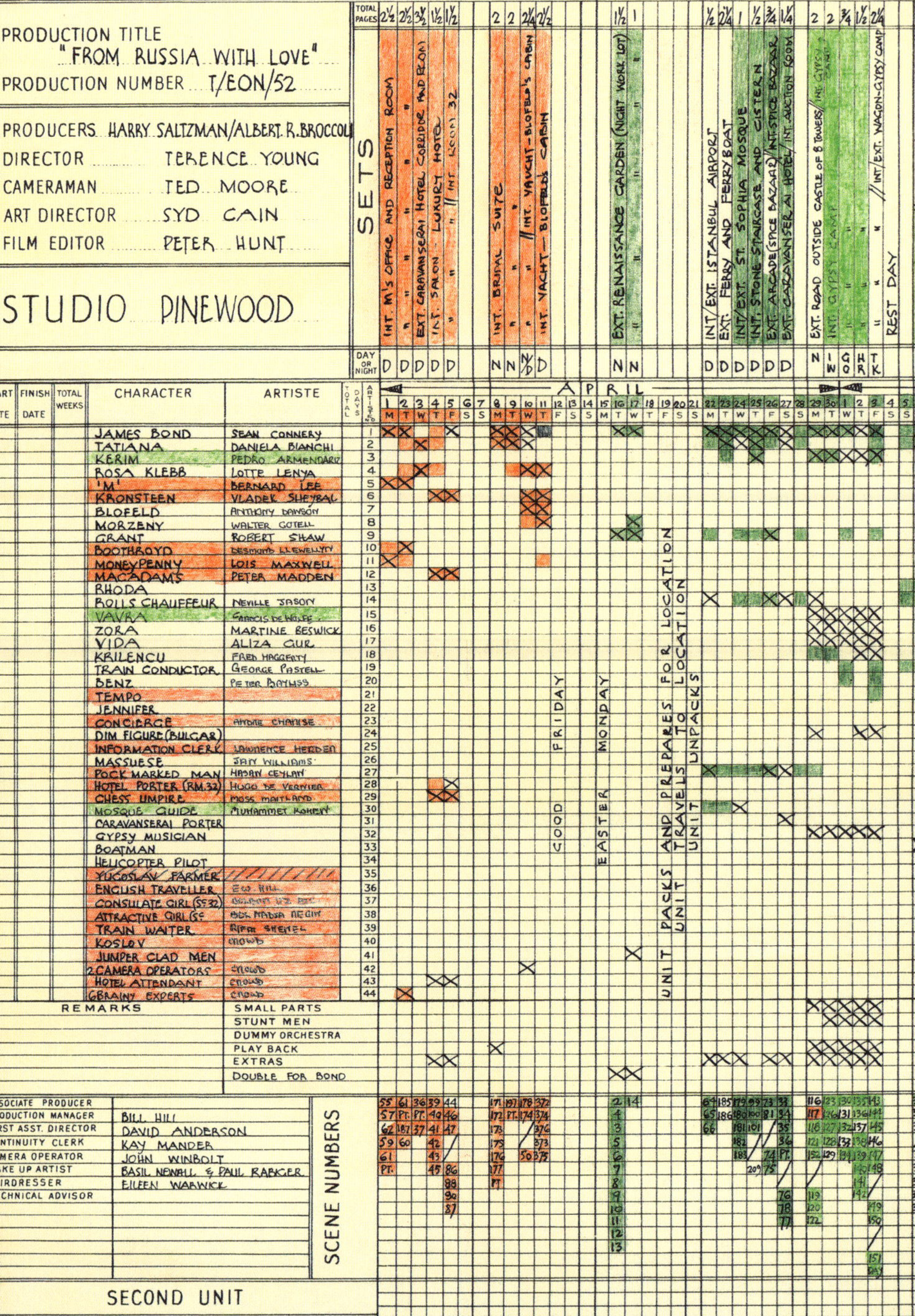
B&W / COLOUR
CRC
PRODUCTION TITLE "FROM RUSSIA WITH LOVE"
PRODUCTION NUMBER T/EON/52
PRODUCERS HARRY SALTZMAN/ALBERT R. BROCCOLI
DIRECTOR TERENCE YOUNG
CAMERAMAN TED MOORE
ART DIRECTOR SYD CAIN
FILM EDITOR PETER HUNT
STUDIO PINEWOOD
SETS
INT. M's OFFICE AND RECEPTION ROOM
EXT. CARAVANSERAI HOTEL CORRIDOR AND ROOM
INT. SALON LUXURY HOTEL
INT. ROOM 32
INT. BRIDAL SUITE
INT. YACHT – BLOFELD's CABIN
EXT. RENAISSANCE GARDEN (NIGHT WORK LOT)
INT/EXT. ISTANBUL AIRPORT
EXT. FERRY AND FERRYBOAT
INT/EXT. ST. SOPHIA MOSQUE
INT. STONE STAIRCASE AND CISTERN
EXT. ARCADE (SPICE BAZAAR) / INT. SPICE BAZAAR
EXT. CARAVANSERAI HOTEL / INT. AUCTION ROOM
EXT. ROAD OUTSIDE CASTLE OF 8 TOWERS / INT. GYPSY CAMP
INT. GYPSY CAMP
INT/EXT. WAGON-GYPSY CAMP
REST DAY
DAY OR NIGHT
APRIL
CHARACTER
ARTISTE
JAMES BOND – SEAN CONNERY
TATIANA – DANIELA BIANCHI
KERIM – PEDRO ARMENDARIZ
ROSA KLEBB – LOTTE LENYA
'M' – BERNARD LEE
KRONSTEEN – VLADEK SHEYBAL
BLOFELD – ANTHONY DAWSON
MORZENY – WALTER GOTELL
GRANT – ROBERT SHAW
BOOTHROYD – DESMOND LLEWELYN
MONEYPENNY – LOIS MAXWELL
MACADAMS – PETER MADDEN
RHODA
ROLLS CHAUFFEUR – NEVILLE JASON
VAVRA – FRANCIS DE WOLFE
ZORA – MARTINE BESWICK
VIDA – ALIZA GUR
KRILENCU – FRED HAGGERTY
TRAIN CONDUCTOR – GEORGE PASTELL
BENZ – PETER BAYLISS
TEMPO
JENNIFER
CONCIERGE – ANDRE CHARISSE
DIM FIGURE (BULGAR)
INFORMATION CLERK – LAWRENCE HERDER
MASSUESE – JAN WILLIAMS
POCK MARKED MAN – HASAN CEYLAN
HOTEL PORTER (RM.32) – HUGO DE VERNIER
CHESS UMPIRE – MOSS MAITLAND
MOSQUE GUIDE – MUHAMMET KOHEN
CARAVANSERAI PORTER
GYPSY MUSICIAN
BOATMAN
HELICOPTER PILOT
YUGOSLAV FARMER
ENGLISH TRAVELLER
CONSULATE GIRL (SS32)
ATTRACTIVE GIRL
TRAIN WAITER
KOSLOV – CROWD
JUMPER CLAD MEN
2 CAMERA OPERATORS – CROWD
HOTEL ATTENDANT – CROWD
6 BRAINY EXPERTS – CROWD
GOOD FRIDAY
EASTER MONDAY
UNIT PACKS AND PREPARES FOR LOCATION
UNIT TRAVELS TO LOCATION
UNIT UNPACKS
REMARKS
SMALL PARTS
STUNT MEN
DUMMY ORCHESTRA
PLAY BACK
EXTRAS
DOUBLE FOR BOND
ASSOCIATE PRODUCER
PRODUCTION MANAGER – BILL HILL
FIRST ASST. DIRECTOR – DAVID ANDERSON
CONTINUITY CLERK – KAY MANDER
CAMERA OPERATOR – JOHN WINBOLT
MAKE UP ARTIST – BASIL NEWALL & PAUL RABIGER
HAIRDRESSER – EILEEN WARWICK
TECHNICAL ADVISOR
SCENE NUMBERS
SECOND UNIT